THE WORLD TAKES

TRENTON MAKES

D0860502

NJ

Bethlehem
Allentown
Reading
Lebanon
PHILADELPHIA
Lancaster
Wilmington
York
Baltimore

NEW

SALT WATER

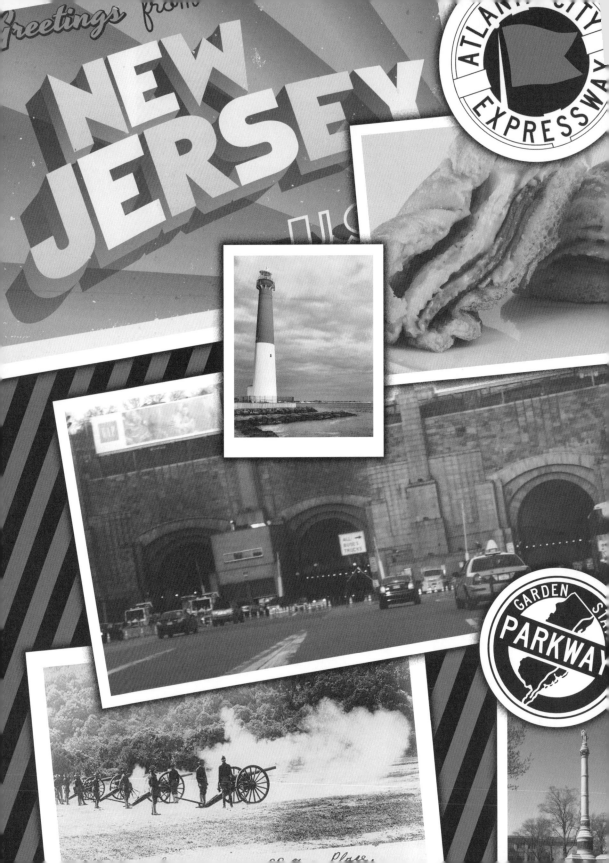

THE

PORK ROLL

Cookbook

We dedicate this book to Joe Bulger and the entire Bulger family for introducing pork roll to Cider Mill Press!

The Pork Roll Cookbook

Copyright 2015 by Appleseed Press Book Publishers LLC
This is an officially licensed book by Cider Mill Press Book Publishers LLC.
All rights reserved under the Pan-American and International Copyright Conventions.

13-Digit ISBN: 978-1-60433-536-1
10-Digit ISBN: 1-60433-536-X

This book may be ordered by mail from the publisher. Please include $4.95 for postage and handling. Please support your local bookseller first!

Books published by Cider Mill Press Book Publishers are available at special discounts for bulk purchases in the United States by corporations, institutions, and other organizations. For more information, please contact the publisher.

Cider Mill Press Book Publishers
"Where good books are ready for press"
12 Spring Street
PO Box 454
Kennebunkport, Maine 04046

Visit us on the Web! www.cidermillpress.com

Design by Jon Chaiet

Shutterstock images used under license

Wikipedia images on pages 4, 7, 8, 11, 14, 16, 18, 19, 21, 22, 28, 34, 36, 39, 40, and 42 used under GNU Free Documentation License.

Library of Congress: p. 8, historical photo of New Jersey National Guard training camp, LC-USZ62-61219.

Printed in the United States of America

1 2 3 4 5 6 7 8 9 0

First Edition

THE
PORK
ROLL
Cookbook

JENNA PIZZI AND SUSAN SPRAGUE YESKE

CIDER MILL PRESS

BOOK PUBLISHERS

KENNEBUNKPORT, MAINE

CONTENTS

INTRODUCTION

FOR MOST WHO COME FROM NEW JERSEY, THERE IS A CLEAR DIVISION BETWEEN NORTH JERSEY AND SOUTH JERSEY. The division is clearly seen on television screens depending on which news stations are broadcast to your home—New York or Philadelphia—or which sports teams you root for. But one thing that unites the state is pork roll.

The iconic, salty breakfast meat has graced the plates of New Jerseyans for more than 150 years and has become a symbol of the region. Those who have moved far away crave the local meat and either look for a way to have it shipped to where they are or come home often enough for a taste.

Like asking, "What's your exit?" when meeting someone from the Garden State, pork roll is a common way to make a connection with someone from the region. There is a raging debate over the name with Northerners referring to the sweet meat as "Taylor Ham" and those who hail from Central and Southern New Jersey calling it "Pork Roll." The "correct name" is debatable and often debated when individuals from the two sides meet.

The New Jersey product has reached into some parts of New York and Connecticut and is popular in parts of Pennsylvania but has never spread much further on the East Coast. To many pork roll lovers, this regionalization

PORK ROLL SLICES

are cut about 1/2 inch thick and the roll has a diameter of 3 1/2 inches for a total of 11 square inches of meaty deliciousness.

is inexplicable. It makes one wonder why wouldn't others want to get in on the meaty goodness that is biting into an everything bagel with a slab of pork roll slathered with egg and American cheese?

Although marketers tried to facilitate, the trend never anchored much past New Jersey and the surrounding states. Producers will ship the meat out to other parts of the country, but it is not on supermarket shelves or marketed to the meat-eating public outside of the mid-Atlantic.

Everyone has a preference on how to cut, cook, and serve pork roll. Usually your thick or thin preference and what you eat alongside your pork roll has a lot to do with how your mom or grandmother served it when you were a child.

Outside supermarkets, pork roll can be found on the menu of most New Jersey diners—of which there are many! It is also a staple in delis and food trucks that sprinkle the state, feeding the "Jersey Breakfast" from Bergen to Atlantic counties.

It is challenging to find pork roll on a menu not paired with egg and cheese, but adventurous foodies obsessed with pork roll have begun experimenting. It has been placed on top of burgers, covered in bacon, chopped up into a taco, cubed and sprinkled on pizza, and baked with sweet pineapple.

PORK ROLL IS PRODUCED IN TRENTON, NEW JERSEY,

the state's capital, by two companies: Taylor Provisions and Case's Pork Roll. Sometimes the product is sold under different names or made for different companies, like Shop Rite brand.

TRENTON MAKES THE WORLD TAKES

THE HISTORY OF PORK ROLL

LIKE THE FLAVOR OF THE MEAT, PORK ROLL'S HISTORY IN CENTRAL NEW JERSEY IS RICH, DATING BACK TO THE FIRST SETTLEMENTS AND COLONIAL DAYS. Throughout the centuries, the way the product has been sold has changed as outdoor markets were forced indoors after a rise of concern for food safety and as corner groceries made way for large supermarkets. But it could still be sold at a restaurant marketed as an authentic product of historic New Jersey.

T he history of the pork roll is very much the history of the two companies best known for producing it: Taylor Provision Company and Case's Pork Roll. Both have been in business for more than 150 years and have dominated the pork roll industry in the United States.

The two companies emerged prior to adequate refrigeration. Back then, when meat could not be purchased from a local farmer, locals purchased cured meat, especially pork, for their families. Salt curing was the easiest and most commonly used way to cure pork meat.

Although large Midwestern cities like Cincinnati and Chicago soon became known for pork production, Trenton's own pork roll processers held their own in the local market, continually producing their pork roll product for decades.

TAYLOR PROVISION COMPANY

Pork roll got its official start in 1856 when the Taylor Provision Company set up shop in Trenton. John Taylor formed the company and started churning out the cured pork treat. He called it Taylor Ham.

The Taylor Provision Company continues in a production facility and office on Perrine Avenue in Trenton. Red-painted buildings occupy most of the block like a fortress to the processed meat delicacy they produce. While Trenton is no longer a major manufacturing center for rubber, wire rope, ceramics, and cigars, pork roll remains.

A TRUE JERSEY RENAISSANCE MAN, *John Taylor was involved in much more than founding a pork roll empire. Taylor was also a state legislator, helped to build the Trenton Battle Monument, which still stands tall above the city today, and ran the Trenton Opera House.*

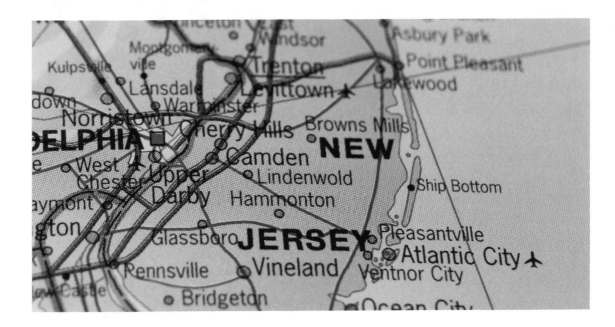

The taste and methods of creating the meat have not changed much over the past 150 years. Taylor is still making the product in much the same way that John Taylor and his predecessors did.

Even before John Taylor made the pork roll, sold in thick logs cured in cloth bags, his ancestors were perfecting the recipe.

The Taylor company traces its lineage back to before the founding of the state of New Jersey when Samuel Taylor set foot in New Jersey after sailing all the way from Derby County, England, in 1677. Landing at Burlington City, Taylor settled an area on what is known today as Crosswick's Creek in Chesterfield, New Jersey.

But it was the grandson of Samuel Taylor, John Taylor, who originated the recipe. He started with a minced ham and eventually perfected it into what is now known as Taylor Pork Roll.

John Taylor began selling the ham to taverns in Trenton, and travelers passing through town on their way to New York and Philadelphia began asking for the meat.

During the American Revolution, John Taylor was called into action, and it was John Taylor's grandson, who bore his grandfather's name, who founded Taylor Provisions Company.

The younger John Taylor was born in 1836 and would

eventually become a state senator. At just eighteen, Taylor, who was looking to earn money for his family, became partner in a grocery store where he worked. He eventually started his own grocery on Green Street in Trenton, which is known today as North Broad Street. Taylor sold his pork roll from his grocery, which became known for the meat.

Well known in the community, Taylor became a state senator, and in 1880 the senate legislative manual recorded his life story for the record. It noted that Taylor founded the Taylor Opera House in 1867 on Trenton's Broad Street downtown, entertaining the 80,000 city residents and those who came in from the neighboring towns in New Jersey and across the Delaware River in Yardley, Pennsylvania.

The theater was listed as an attraction in several editions of the *Julius Cahn Official Theatrical Guide*, a reference of theaters along travel routes and rail lines in the United States and Canada. Prices at the theater ranged from a quarter to a dollar, according to a listing for the theater in the 1903-1904 edition of the guide. And Taylor Opera House had more seats than the other theater in town, the State Street Theatre. With the advent of film, the Opera House was transformed into a movie theater dubbed the Capitol Theatre. The theater closed in 1972 and has since been demolished. (And yet, the pork roll continues on!)

Prior to his term as a senator, Taylor served as a local elected official in Trenton and was behind the elimination of the outdoor markets along North Broad Street. The move to have food purveyors pushed inside to closed areas was meant to make a more sanitary environment for distributors and consumers alike.

When John Taylor's son William Taylor took over the family business, he too, faced further regulations regarding safety.

In 1906, the Federal Meat Inspection Act was passed, regulating the slaughter of animals, the processing of meat, and, more importantly to Taylor, requiring the exact labeling of all meat and meat food products.

Taylor proudly peddled the name Taylor Ham, which was problematic because the product was pork, not ham. Rebranding as Pork Roll didn't hurt business, however. With a flair for the dramatic, William Taylor took to advertising his product in grandiose shows of frivolity.

In the early 1900s Taylor established what was known at the time as the tallest advertisement on the

Pennsylvania railroad—a gigantic pork roll towering over the tracks in the New Jersey Meadows.

During the summer when thousands took to the Jersey shore for the fresh, sea-salt air and sun, Taylor too was there with his adverts. Balloons emblazoned with the Taylor name floated off-shore but in sight of the visitors strolling casually on the boardwalk.

Flexing his pocketbook, Taylor also organized what was called the most expensive advertisement in the world. He employed acrobats to spread the Taylor brand at the Trenton State Fair. It is said that Taylor had two large Taylor balloons that floated above as acrobats performed below during the event.

William Taylor died in 1940, and the company was passed down to his grandson John Taylor Crumbler. A descendant of Crumbler's still heads the business to this day.

CASE'S PORK ROLL

Although Taylor Provisions Company can claim to be the first pork roll company, Case's Pork Roll is another longtime favorite with a long history. Case's was founded in 1870 by George Washington Case, a former butcher who started production from his hog farm in Belle Mead, New Jersey.

George Washington Case also manufactured feed for cattle and was the originator of an ointment for horses made from herbs and meat byproducts. But Case stuck with the pork product that would one day be known in most every New Jersey household.

Case began peddling his smoked and salted pork roll from a cart and rivaled Trenton native Taylor for customers.

In 1909, Case moved his business to Trenton, where he opened a store on Passaic Street, sparking a cross-town rivalry with Taylor Provisions that still smolders to this day. Although the Case's Pork Roll production location moved around a bit throughout the years, the pork roll has continually been manufactured in Trenton ever since.

Andrew Jackson Case, the son of the business' founder, developed the first summer pork roll in 1930, opening up the ability to produce more and more pork roll. Prior to 1930, pork roll was manufactured only in the fall and winter when weather was best for curing the meats. But, with the advent of refrigeration, the company was able to keep the meat cool and away from moisture in the air as it cured.

In addition to pork roll, the sons of George Washington Case were very involved in promoting baseball in Trenton. George Washington Case Jr. was a professional baseball player with the Washington Senators and the Cleveland Indians, and he and his brothers arranged exhibition games in Trenton with many of the best-known baseball players of the time. Andrew Jackson Case brought stars such as

IN ADDITION TO PORK ROLL, *the Case family was popular in Trenton for baseball. George Washington Case Jr. made it to the big leagues playing for the Washington Senators and Cleveland Indians.*

CASE'S PORK ROLL *was once an icon on the boardwalks along New Jersey beaches.*

Babe Ruth and Lou Gehrig to Trenton for the games. Case later became the owner of the Trenton Senators baseball team, which played at Dunn Field near the Brunswick Traffic Circle.

In the 1960s, Case's Pork Roll began seeing demand for pork roll outside of its regular distribution area. Although the demand was not enough to spread distribution to the far reaches of the county where former Trentonians had relocated, the company began shipping pork roll out to their hungry customers at special request. According to an article from *Trenton* magazine in 1965, the company mailed the meat as far away as Korea.

In 2012, the Case's Pork Roll factory in the Chambersburg section of Trenton suffered a fire that left a smoky smell of cooked meat lingering in the air throughout the city. The three-alarm blaze tore through the roof of the factory and took two ovens out of commission, temporarily halting production at the factory. But the fire didn't take the company out.

Today Case's is run by Tom Greib, son of Arleen Greib, the daughter of a Case—Russell Case, to be exact. The factory continues to crank out meaty pork roll—both tangy and mild—under the Case's name as well as other labels to be sold at supermarkets.

CHAPTER 2

A PORCINE PARTY

SOME THINGS ARE JUST BIGGER THAN ANTICIPATED—AND ONE OF THOSE WAS THE FIRST TRENTON PORK ROLL FESTIVAL IN 2013. Meat-lovers packed into the rear parking lot at the Trenton Social bar on South Broad Street in Trenton. With more than four thousand people stopping by throughout the 12-hour festival, there was a line just to get in. The skies opened up and rain and hail fell as festival-goers scattered to find cover—twice. And even that didn't put much damper on the porcine party.

The six-member blues band The Pork Roll Project from Philadelphia was one of the acts that kept the tunes going throughout the day. Adults sampled local brews like Riverhorse Brewery's libations available in the beer garden, and kids got their faces painted. Festival merchandise included t-shirts proclaiming love of pork roll.

But the crowning moment—literally—was the first "Miss Pork Roll" pageant.

MISS PORK ROLL QUEEN

"Sunny side up egg, two slices of pork roll and cheddar cheese," says Maggie Kowalski of Bayonne.

Growing up in Hudson County, Kowalski grew up having pork roll for breakfast, although she called it Taylor Ham, the name the meaty treat is given in New Jersey's northern regions.

The 27-year-old still eats her pork roll on a bulkie breakfast sandwich, although she is experimenting adding the meat product into other recipes too, including experimenting with a pork roll chili.

After all, she is the first Miss Pork Roll.

Kowalski was one of six women who were chosen as finalists in the Miss Pork Roll competition at the first Trenton Pork Roll Festival. Being a new festival and a competition never before attempted, Kowalski didn't know quite what to expect.

"I just went in and my strategy was to have fun and not take it too seriously," she said. "I had no idea that I was going to win because everybody who competed had something totally different. No two girls were the same."

The contest was very close, with only a few votes separating Kowalski from runner-up Stephanee Brown.

> **THE FIRST-EVER TRENTON PORK ROLL FESTIVAL WAS HELD ON MAY 25, 2014 CELEBRATING THE HOME-TOWN MEAT MADE IN NEW JERSEY'S CAPITAL CITY.**

THE FINALISTS IN THE FIRST MISS PORK ROLL PAGEANT INCLUDED A DRAG QUEEN.

For the talent portion, Brown told a heart-warming story about her grandfather and their love for pork roll.

But Kowalski won the hearts and votes of festival-goers by challenging a guy to a pushup contest. Kowalski later said she wanted to prove that loving pork roll or being crowned Miss Pork Roll Queen did not mean being fat or not physically fit. Proving that she was "Jersey Strong" won her the title, which she said would hopefully somehow turn into a chance to meet New Jersey's own Bon Jovi.

Since her win, Kowalski said not much has changed day to day except that people she knows call her by the title of Miss Pork Roll Queen every once in a while.

"My boyfriend thinks it is the coolest thing in the world," she said. "At work they refer to me as Miss Pork Roll Queen."

When first telling people about her title, Kowalski said some people get the "deer in headlights" look and don't know how to respond.

Nevertheless, Kowalski is, well, Jersey Proud.

"If you come to my apartment, the sash is hanging on the door to my office," she said.

THE MAN WITH THE PLAN

The plan for the pork roll festival was hatched not out of a love for pork roll but instead in looking for a festival that would celebrate the city of Trenton.

Back in 2013, marketing specialist Scott Miller saw that much of the news about Trenton was a downer. As owner and principal of Exit 7A Creative Services, a production and marketing studio specializing in audio, video, photography and social media services, Miller consults for local events and businesses. But he wanted to work on something independently that could be good for the city.

What stuck with him, Miller said, was the iconic bridge that spans the Delaware River connecting New Jersey's capitol to Morrisville, Pennsylvania. In large neon letters, the bridge reads TRENTON MAKES THE WORLD TAKES—homage to Trenton's days as a production hub for goods as varied as fine china and wire rope for suspension bridges like the Golden Gate Bridge.

Many of those factories have long been closed, either torn down to make way for some new redevelopment project or left as a shell, monuments to the city's industrial age.

But one industry has kept production in Trenton as others moved away or shut down: pork roll. Both the Taylor Provisions Company and Case's Pork Roll factories are humming along, tractor trailers pulling off

every day to bring the tasty treat to hungry customers at stores all over the region.

"I thought it would be nice if we could have a big festival and we could tie it to what is our largest ongoing industry here," Miller said. "It just seemed logical."

Growing up in Wilkes-Barre, Pennsylvania, Miller never got to experience pork roll.

"I don't know if we even had pork roll growing up there," he said.

But then a friend from Trenton brought over a few boxes of pork roll and started cooking.

"I said, 'That smells just like bacon,'" Miller remembered. "That smoke flavor just hit my nose and, you know, I don't really even like ham but it smelled so good."

When he created a Facebook group to see if the public would readily accept a Pork Roll Festival, nearly 3,000 people joined the group and many offered to help. That is where Miller hooked up with TC Nelson, owner of the Trenton Social Bar and Restaurant on South Broad Street, who offered to host the event at his place.

After that, Miller gave himself just three months to plan the event.

"I hired all local musicians mostly people that rehearse in my studio," he said. The acts ranged from jazz, blues, indie bands and rock.

From there the idea took off larger than Miller or Nelson had expected.

Miller estimates he only spent about $30 on advertising the event; the rest was just grassroots and viral with friends inviting friends to come.

Thinking he was putting together an event that would fill the restaurant, small beer

PEOPLE CAME TO THE FIRST PORK ROLL FESTIVAL *from as far away as Alaska, South Carolina, and Toronto, Canada.*

garden, and rear parking lot, Miller said he didn't think the event would have the wide-ranging appeal that it did.

"I didn't know how passionate about it people would be," Miller said. "It really blew me away. People got on planes and traveled here. That is crazy, you know, for a log of meat."

The success of the event has Miller confident that pork roll could be a catalyst for revitalizing the city of Trenton. He's thinking about a campaign to make pork roll popular to people outside the area.

To advertise the meat's prominence in Trenton, restaurants could have a sticker saying that they "proudly serve Trenton pork roll."

"I really think that it could help revive the city," Miller said. "Something stupid and silly like that."

EMERGENCY PORK ROLL DELIVERY

During that first Pork Roll Festival, vendors served up about 1,200 pounds of pork roll.

And they nearly ran out.

TC Nelson of Trenton Social called on a friend who works at Case's Pork Roll to bring by additional logs of pork roll to be baked, grilled, toasted, sliced, diced, chopped and put into the different kinds of food being sold during the day-long party.

Outside, people waited for more than an hour at some of the food trucks serving one-of-a-kind pork roll specialties.

Inside, Trenton Social was serving up traditional pork roll egg and cheese sandwiches on Trenton's own Italian People's Bakery rolls. For the slightly more adventurous, there was an approachable feast they called the Trenton Burger, a beef burger topped with a grilled slice of pork roll. Or you could get a taco with tender pulled pork inside comingling with salty, diced pieces of pork roll topped with sour pickled radishes, pickled onion and Swiss cheese.

PORK ROLL SUSHI?
PORK ROLL GELATO?

New Jersey sushi chef Charlie Yeh is always thinking about food and new, innovative ideas to incorporate different ingredients into his menu at Sumo Sushi in Pennington, New Jersey. One thing the Taiwan native was not expecting was to be asked to use pork roll in his sushi.

Yeh draws in a large crowd at Trenton Social with his sushi nights. So, when Trenton Social restaurant owner TC Nelson, hosted the first Trenton Pork Roll Festival, he asked Yeh to help serve up some new and different pork roll varieties for the event.

At first, Yeh was unsure exactly what he was going to serve.

"It was challenging for me because we don't use that

MANY THINGS FROM TRENTON, *including many people, have migrated to nearby Hamilton Township. Catering to former Trentonians and lovers of pork roll, the Jersey Girl Café has opened three locations in Hamilton, serving up pork roll in several different dishes including a Jersey Chef Salad with pork roll, American cheese, red onion, tomato, and cucumber. Pork roll also comes as an add-on to any sandwich served at the café.*

for cooking," Yeh said.

But then Yeh made a connection with the salty, cured meat and the way fish was once salt packed to preserve it over time. Yeh explained that traditionally sushi also included this salted variety of fish, so he treated the pork roll as if it were fish.

"It is the same idea, the same concept," Yeh said.

He cut the pork roll into small strips and seared the pork roll for just a minute or two. Inside the sushi roll he added avocado and cucumber to go alongside the meat. To top things off in a creative way, Yeh substituted the crunchy breadcrumbs that often top sushi in restaurants with a deep fried slice of pork roll. Cutting the pork roll very thin using a mandolin, Yeh deep fried the pork roll chips until they were very crispy. Before adding them to the dish, Yeh crumbled the chips on top of the "sushi" roll and served it up to interested and adventurous eaters.

"It is like an East meets West thing," he said.

In addition to his restaurant Sumo Sushi, Yeh runs Viva Gelato, where he crafts unique flavors of smooth, Italian gelato. During the day, Viva Gelato also serves breakfast, including pork roll, egg, and cheese sandwiches. This all came together in something truly unique at the festival: Pork Roll Gelato, served with a chocolate-covered piece of pork roll inside.

"It tasted pretty good because it was sweet and salty," Yeh said.

It's that creativity that keeps the restaurant industry fresh—and that brings pork roll into so many new recipes and flavors.

CHAPTER 3
PORK ROLL TODAY

WHAT, YOU'VE NEVER HAD PORK ROLL?! PORK ROLL IS LIKE CANADIAN BACON, BUT CHEWIER. It has that cured, salty taste that makes bacon so great with eggs and coffee but with no portions that are pure fat or gristle. The fat is redistributed in such a way that pork roll is buttery and sweeter.

The meat is usually cut about 1/4-inch thick—that's how thick the companies make their pre-packaged slices. Most people prefer more than one slice on their pork roll, egg, and cheese sandwich.

We can describe pork roll all day, but what you need to do is smell it frying up. You'll salivate.

In New Jersey, New York, and parts of Pennsylvania, pork roll can generally be found at grocery stores or supermarkets in the meat section near the hot dogs and sausages.

Wholesale, the meat is sold in unsliced rolls of 1 pound, 1.5 pounds, and 3 pounds as well was 6-ounce boxes containing quarter-inch vacuum-sealed slices of pork roll ready to go on the griddle.

In addition to the grocery store's refrigerated section, pork roll can be found at local meat markets and most places that serve breakfast in New Jersey including coffee shops, cafes, food trucks, and, most importantly, diners.

After all, New Jersey, with restaurants dotting the many highways and byways of the state, is known as the diner capital.

Pork roll pre-dates even diners.

Pork roll got its official start in 1856 when the Taylor Provision Company set up shop in Trenton. And diners first appeared in New Jersey in 1912 in the form of the "lunch wagon"—think: horse-drawn food truck.

According to The History of Diners in New Jersey by New Jersey journalist Peter Genovese, the wagons provided meals for working men on the go and eventually also provided late night lunches. The lunch wagons eventually morphed into the New Jersey diners known for making eggs and other breakfast specialties—including pork roll—quickly, on the cheap, and at all hours of the day and night.

TRADE SECRETS

Today, Case's Pork Roll produces two different varieties of the regional delicacy: mild and tangy. The tangy meat is made so by a lactic acid in the meat that gives it the distinct flavor. The tangier of the two is the original product of Cloverdell, which was founded by Russel Case. Case's merged with Cloverdell in 1947, and that's when the two plants founded by different Case men became one.

Both companies have heavily guarded the secrets behind the mysteriously delicious meat product, describing the recipes as trade secrets.

Despite this secrecy, the basic ingredients and production steps are public knowledge. The meat that is shipped to Trenton to make its way into the pork roll to make the meaty delicacy is usually low in fat—between 85 and 90 percent lean. It is salt cured with a mix of secret

"**BORN IN TRENTON IN 1856,** this supersalty, compulsively edible precooked pork sausage is the unofficial state meat of New Jersey and the pride of Garden State natives like Prune's Gabrielle Hamilton, who has featured it on her menu."

—New York magazine

THE PORK ROLL COOKBOOK

spices that neither Case nor Taylor will divulge. It is the specific spices that give the pork roll the unique, mouthwatering flavor that fans crave.

After it is seasoned, the meat is hickory smoked, giving it another pungent piece of its distinct flavor.

In fact, Case's manufacturing plant goes through at least 50 pounds of hickory wood from Virginia every night the plant operates, according to current owner Tom Gribe. And Case's is busy making pork roll every weekend, plus some Saturdays, depending on demand. Case's produces about 65,000 pounds of pork roll a year.

Some say there is a distinct difference between the pork roll produced at Case's Pork Roll vs. Taylor Provision Company, while others say it is difficult to distinguish the difference.

The two manufacturers have the same main ingredients listed on the packaging: pork, salt, sugar, and spices. And that leads to only slight variations in the nutritional facts for each.

Case's Pork Roll has slightly more sodium than Taylor Provisions with 450 milligrams as opposed to Taylor's 430 milligrams. Both have 130 calories with 100 calories from fat. Taylor has 12 grams of fat compared to Case's Pork Roll's 11 grams. Case's Pork Roll also has 1 more gram of sugar than Taylor's.

PORK ROLL FOR FOODIES

Although pork roll is difficult to find outside of New Jersey, Philadelphia and parts of New York, some Jersey-native chefs serve up the meat to customers elsewhere—and in creative, new ways.

Mike Isabella, who grew up in Little Ferry, New Jersey but now owns several restaurants in Washington, DC, has put pork roll on several of his menus.

At his sandwich shop called "G," Isabella has crafted a unique take on the "Jersey Breakfast," pork roll,

CHEF CHRIS RITTER

has been known to serve a pork roll, egg, and cheese egg roll at the Grubhouse in Philadelphia.

egg, cheese sandwich. At "G," Isabella has instead a "Jersey Mac" with duck egg, house-made Taylor ham, Muenster cheese, and duck fat English muffins.

At Graffiato in Washington, DC's Chinatown neighborhood, Isabella serves artisanal pizzas, including Hawaiian pizza served with "Taylor Spam," tying together Isabella's New Jersey heritage and love for both Taylor pork roll and Hawaii's Spam.

The alumnus of Bravo's Top Chef and Top Chef All Stars cooking reality shows makes his own pork roll by his own secret recipe in the restaurants. Isabella said he strives to make classic Taylor ham from Virginia-raised pigs.

"It is not difficult to make," Isabella said.

Isabella said he chose to include the New Jersey favorite on his menu because it fits in with the kind of food he strives to make—influenced by his Italian-American heritage but in a fresh, new way. Although pork roll is seen as a diner food, Isabella said he could see the lowly pork roll appear on restaurant menus and in a way appealing to diners outside of New Jersey who might be unfamiliar with the traditional ways of eating the meat.

IN A NEW BRUNSWICK, NJ EPISODE OF "MAN V. FOOD" ON THE TRAVEL CHANNEL,

host Adam Richman tried a Fat Romano: thin steak slices, over-easy egg, Taylor pork roll, French fries, lettuce, and tomatoes.

"I just don't think it is well known outside of New Jersey," Isabella said.

Other foodie restaurants have placed pork roll on their menus—specifically for brunch—most making a version of the product themselves and serving it up with egg and cheese, but with a twist.

At Philadelphia's Amis, owned by Philadelphia restaurant royalty Marc Vetri, pork roll is the draw in the Jersey Cannonball sandwich. It's served with a sunnyside-up egg and cheese on a bun with pickled red pepper relish.

Some daring home cooks have attempted to make their own pork roll at home, either because they are adventurous and curious if it can be done, or they live outside of the area and are seeking an alternative to shipping New Jersey's signature meat.

Chefs have individual recipes and variations, but the basics are the same. The pork meat—usually shoulder or ham—is ground, sometimes accompanied by other cuts of meat, and combined with spices and curing agents. Then the pork roll is cased, either in a cloth bag or sausage casing, and dried before it is hickory smoked and cooled. Then it is sliced, grilled, and ready to eat.

"THE SANDWICH FROM MASTORIS

[Greek mega-diner in Bordentown] comes with three thick slices of pork roll, each one slit inwards from their outer edge to allow it to stay flat as it shrinks while it cooks on a flat griddle. This is a common practice known to all pork roll aficionados, and the resulting shapes are referred to variously the 'fireman's badge' cut or the 'Pac Man' cut."

—J. Kenji Lopez-Alt, managing culinary director at SeriousEats.com

CHAPTER 4

A NEW JERSEY THING

PORK ROLL HAS BECOME A CULTURAL TOUCHSTONE TO THOSE FROM THE REGION AND SOMETHING THAT MANY PEOPLE OFTEN MISS WHEN THEY MOVE AWAY. "It is just a New Jersey thing," said Tom Gribe, the current owner of Case's Pork Roll. "It's just always been a regional item," he said. "I don't think I really appreciated pork roll until I saw that it was something you couldn't just go to the grocery store and buy," said Miss Pork Roll Maggie Kowalski, who went out of state for college. "I had known from 17 years of experience that I can go to the Shop Rite and get pork roll and have it for breakfast."

**A**lthough she was disappointed not to be able to cure her college hangovers with a bit of pork roll paired with egg and cheese for a comforting Sunday morning breakfast, Kowalski soon found that it was a bond when she met someone else from the New Jersey region that could commiserate with her urge for the food. "You create a bond with a stranger," Kowalksi said.

When she came home from school, pork roll made it onto a list of priority items that must be done in the short window of time in the Garden State, Kowalski said.

"It was one of the top five things I needed," Kowalksi said. "A sunny side up egg, two slices of pork roll and cheddar cheese."

Trenton Pork Roll Festival founder Scott Miller didn't grow up on pork roll, and at first he thought it was a guy thing. He was surprised to see how the festival attracted whole families.

"It brings back memories of grandparents, especially for New Jersey ex-patriots," he said. "It is something they miss as a food stuff, but it also really brings them back to their childhood and the things that they miss. I think that is really what we tap into with the pork roll festival. It is something about the aroma and the flavor and the childhood memories meld together to make something magical."

TC Nelson, who hosted the festival at his bar Trenton

> ## "PEOPLE WHO DON'T KNOW ANY BETTER THINK IT'S GRILLED BOLOGNA,
> *but it is a totally unique product whose pinkness seems to grow as it pops and crackles cooking in a pan. ... When I was a child, Taylor Pork Roll stands seemed to be everywhere, stretching from Sandy Hook to Cape May, and they were visited not only by Garden Staters, but Philadelphia vacationers jamming the Jersey Shore."*
>
> —Frederick N. Rasmussen, Baltimore Sun

Social, was previously the owner of a bagel shop and cafe in Trenton, serving up lots and lots of pork roll, egg, and cheese sandwiches every day.

He guesses the regional exclusivity of pork roll is part of the draw. Growing up in New Jersey, he remembers his uncle coming back for visits with pork roll cravings.

"Jersey tomatoes, Tastykakes, and pork roll," Nelson said. "That's what he wanted."

Len Boccassini, a freelance culinary journalist and blogger at FoodiDude.com, was born in Hoboken, New Jersey, and raised in Bergen County. When he moved out to central Pennsylvania a few years ago he was horrified to learn that his go-to breakfast meat was no longer readily available in the supermarket or grocery store.

"I would look for Taylor ham and it was nowhere to be found," Boccassini said. "It was just so odd."

Boccassini said he knew that the breakfast meat wasn't available in far-away states, but in Harrisburg he was living only a few hours from the home of pork roll.

"It is just amazing," Boccassini said. "It is just astounding. A three-hour drive in any direction and they haven't a clue."

"It really is a food of local orientation," Boccassini

describes comparing it to local culinary favorites that are enjoyed by individuals in a very specific area elsewhere in the country.

"It just boggles my mind that something so popular hasn't at least invaded the surrounding states," Boccassini said, adding that he has seen it on menus in Philadelphia.

Now that Boccassini has moved back to New Jersey, picking up Taylor Ham is easy again. When foodie friends visit, he makes sure they try the traditional pork roll, egg, and cheese sandwich he holds so fondly in his taste memory.

Foodies tend to be interested in pork roll because of its affiliation with diner food.

"These dives, these greasy spoons, they were looked down upon as second-class food," he said. "But now it is almost like a cult movie following. They are never going to win an Oscar for these movies but they have never been more popular."

John Yarusi has been eating pork roll since his mother served it up for breakfast.

"Pork roll, egg, and cheese in a classic way," he said. "It's just got to be in my blood. It was our comfort food."

He really missed pork roll when he went to graduate school in Idaho.

But now, as owner of Johnny's Pork Roll Truck, he's surrounded by it.

Wherever he goes, people wave, and smile at the Pork Roll truck bearing the name of New Jersey's meat, "the Springsteen of food," he adds.

"They want to take pictures," Yarusi said. "I am amazed that I am the only one around."

Yarusi said he likes to take risks on things like a pork roll Ruben, pork roll grilled cheese or a pork roll Cuban sandwich. He also has a BLT-like sandwich with pork roll, bacon, lettuce, and tomato. The Hawaiian

sandwich has pork roll and sweet pineapple. Another has a duck egg and Gruyere cheese.

"I have made pork roll split pea soup, pork roll Bolognese," Yarusi said rattling off a few more of his creations. "Anything sweet and salty to me works so well."

Pork roll is the great equalizer, bringing together all New Jersey folks.

"Country club people eat it," Yarusi said. "I do stuff for Morgan Stanley, they will have us bring stuff there for the traders. They all eat it. The guy that takes your garbage eats it. The guy who owns the garbage truck eats it."

> "BUT IF YOUR GRANDMOTHER'S FRIDGE ALWAYS HELD A BURLAP-WRAPPED ROLL OF TAYLOR HAM (also known as Taylor pork roll), or after a night of bar-hopping in Belmar you staggered into the OB Diner for Taylor ham, egg and cheese on a roll, you understand the Garden State's passion for pork roll."
>
> —Beverly Savage, New York Times

HOW TO BUY PORK ROLL OUT OF STATE

Craving pork roll, but living in the South, West, Midwest, or Northeast? Others in the same predicament have led the way for many companies who specialize in shipping pork roll (and sometimes with other local delicacies) to hungry former residents of the Garden State, no matter where they are. Pork roll products can also be found online for purchase at Amazon.com.

JERSEY BOY PORK ROLL: Jersey Boy Pork Roll ships both Taylor Provisions products as well as Case's Pork Roll products in different sizes and quantities. The pork roll shipping company was founded by national talk radio host Bruce Williams, who is originally from New Jersey but later in life moved to Florida. Pork roll can be ordered online at their website JerseyBoyPorkRoll.com or by phone at 732-297-4798.

JERSEY PORK ROLL: Jersey Pork Roll opened its Internet store shipping pork roll and other local treats around the country in 2004. The wholesaler, based in Piscataway, sells only Taylor Provisions brand and under its alternative name Trenton Pork Roll. The pork roll is also sold in combo packs with products such as Sabrett Hot Dogs and Scrapple. The store also sells local favorites like Tastycakes as well as gifts like t-shirts and ornaments featuring pork roll or the Jersey Shore. The products can be ordered online at JerseyPorkRoll.com or by phone at 1-866-4NJ-PORK

CASE'S PORK ROLL STORE: The Case's Pork Roll Store is affiliated with Case's Pork Roll and sells only Case's Pork Roll Products, shipping them across the United States. The pork roll is sold in varying quantities, including 1.5-pound, 3-pound, and 6-pound bags, and 9-pound boxes of sliced pork roll, which comes out to about 144 slices. Orders can be processed online at CasePorkRollStore.com or by phone at 1-888-996-7833.

THE TAYLOR HAM MAN: The Taylor Ham Man sells Taylor Provisions pork roll products as well as other regional meats, such as Sabrett's hot dogs and Scrapple. Orders can be placed online at TheTaylorHamMan.com or by phone at 973-671-8426.

DELICIOUS ORCHARDS: Delicious Orchards is a country food market with an online store shipping local food and food baskets. In addition to the many local favorites sold online, Delicious Orchards, headquartered in Colts Neck, sells 3-pound bags of Taylor Provisions pork roll. Orders can be placed online at DeliciousOrchardsNJOnline.com.

STARTERS & SNACKS
STARTERS & SNACKS
STARTERS & SNACKS
STARTERS & SNACKS
STARTERS & SNACKS
STARTERS & SNACKS
STARTERS & SNACKS
STARTERS & SNACKS
STARTERS & SNACKS
STARTERS & SNACKS
STARTERS & SNACKS
STARTERS & SNACKS

STARTERS & SNACKS

STARTERS & SNACKS
STARTERS & SNACKS
STARTERS & SNACKS
STARTERS & SNACKS
STARTERS & SNACKS
STARTERS & SNACKS
STARTERS & SNACKS
STARTERS & SNACKS
STARTERS & SNACKS
STARTERS & SNACKS
STARTERS & SNACKS
STARTERS & SNACKS

DEVILED EGGS WITH PORK ROLL

Take traditional deviled eggs up a notch with pork roll.

¼ cup pork roll, chopped small

4 large hard-cooked eggs

2½ tablespoons mayonnaise

1½ teaspoons Dijon mustard

Salt and pepper to taste

Tabasco or hot sauce, if desired

Cooking spray

MAKES 4 SERVINGS

1. Spray skillet with cooking spray, briefly brown pork roll, then remove from skillet to paper towel to drain.

2. Peel eggs, cut in half lengthwise, carefully remove yolks and place in a small bowl. Put egg white halves on a medium-sized plate, cut-side-up.

3. Mash the yolks as much as possible with a fork, then add mayonnaise, mustard, and a few drops of hot sauce, if using. Taste mixture and add salt, pepper, and extra hot sauce as desired.

4. Using a teaspoon, carefully fill the egg whites with the yolk mixture, then sprinkle some pork roll bits over each egg. Serve, or cover with plastic wrap and refrigerate until serving.

JERSEY-STYLE CREAMY DIP

Dip, meet pork roll. Serve with chips, pita chips, carrot and celery sticks—basically, anything you dip.

Cooking spray

3 slices pork roll, diced small

1 cup sour cream

½ cup mayonnaise

4 ounces cream cheese, room temperature

½ cup shredded Cheddar cheese

¼ cup finely chopped onions

Chips, veggie sticks, or other dipping foods

MAKES 4 TO 6 SERVINGS

1. Spray small skillet with cooking spray. Briefly brown chopped pork roll, then remove to paper towel to drain and cool.

2. In a small bowl, combine sour cream, mayonnaise, cream cheese, Cheddar cheese, chopped onion, and pork roll until well mixed.

3. Refrigerate for two hours or up to 1 day before serving. Serve with chips—or carrot and celery sticks if you want to get your veggies in.

VARIATION

FOR A SPICIER VERSION, SOFTEN 1 TABLESPOON CHOPPED JALAPENO PEPPERS (WEAR GLOVES TO CUT PEPPER AND REMOVE SEEDS) WITH THE PORK ROLL.

BAKED POTATO RAFTS WITH PORK ROLL AND CHEESE

Who doesn't love baked potatoes? This simple appetizer combines the natural flavor pairing of pork roll and cheese with the earthiness of a baked potato.

4 baking potatoes, cut into ½-inch-thick rounds //// ¼ cup melted butter	Cooking spray //// 4 slices pork roll, diced small	8 ounces shredded Cheddar cheese //// ½ cup chopped sweet onions

MAKES 4 TO 6 SERVINGS

1. Preheat oven to 400 degrees.

2. Brush both sides of the potato slices with butter and place them on an ungreased cookie sheet. Turning once, bake in the preheated oven for 30 to 40 minutes or until soft inside and lightly browned on the outside.

3. While potatoes are baking, spray small skillet with cooking spray and briefly brown pork roll pieces. Remove from skillet to a paper towel to drain.

4. When potatoes are baked, top with pork, cheese, and onion. Bake for 1 minute longer to melt the cheese.

VARIATION

SERVE WITH A SMALL BOWL OF SOUR CREAM SO YOUR GUESTS CAN ADD A DOLLOP IF THEY WANT.

MAPLE-MUSTARD PORK ROLL BITES

Sweet and spicy, these little bites of heaven will be snatched up by meat lovers and pork roll fans.

1 pound pork roll, cut into 2-inch by 2-inch cubes	⅓ cup maple syrup **////** 1 tablespoon prepared mustard	20 to 24 toothpicks

MAKES 20 TO 24 APPETIZERS

1. Preheat oven to 375 degrees. Place pork roll pieces on a rimmed baking tray. In a small bowl, combine maple syrup and mustard.

2. Bake pork roll for 8 minutes. Brush generously with maple-mustard glaze. Bake for another 8 minutes more or until pork roll is heated through. Insert toothpicks in center of each and move bites to a serving plate.

IN 2009, NEW JERSEY FILMMAKER STEVE CHERNOSKI MADE "NEW JERSEY: THE MOVIE" AND SET OUT TO FIND THE DIVIDING LINE BETWEEN NORTH, SOUTH, AND MAYBE EVEN CENTRAL NEW JERSEY. THE FILM ADDRESSES THE DEBATE BETWEEN TAYLOR HAM AND PORK ROLL. "OUR IDENTITIES REVOLVE AROUND PHILADELPHIA OR NEW YORK CITY," CHERNOSKI SAID IN A 2014 INTERVIEW WITH NJ.COM. "TAYLOR HAM [VS] PORK ROLL IS SOMETHING THAT IS SOLELY OURS. THAT IS WHY WE FIGHT ABOUT IT."

CANDIED PORK ROLL

Move over, candied bacon. Pork roll fans will love this alternative use for their favorite meat that blends sweetness and saltiness.

⅓ to ½ cup brown sugar

½ pound thick-cut pork roll, cut into strips or diced fine if planning to use as garnish

MAKES 1 CUP

1. Heat skillet to medium. Add pork roll pieces to the pan, laying them flat. Sprinkle with some of the brown sugar, then allow brown sugar to melt and meat to begin to brown. Flip and repeat the process, keeping a close eye on the skillet. The candied pork roll is done when it is crisp and caramelized on both sides.

2. Move candied pork roll to parchment paper or wax paper to cool.

3. Serve sprinkled on ice cream or crepes or use to add pizzazz to the tops of frosted cupcakes.

VARIATIONS

SPICE UP THE CANDIED PORK ROLL BY ADDING ½ TEASPOON OF DRIED MUSTARD OR ⅛ TEASPOON BLACK PEPPER TO THE BROWN SUGAR MIXTURE.

WANT WHOLE SLICES OF CANDIED PORK ROLL FOR BREAKFAST? DON'T CUT THE PORK ROLL; JUST CARMELIZE AND SERVE!

PORK ROLL STROMBOLI

You didn't know pork roll was an Italian food?

Cooking spray

¾ cup pork roll, coarsely chopped

16-ounce package frozen bread dough (thawed) or 13.8-ounce can refrigerated pizza crust dough

½ teaspoon dried basil leaves, or two teaspoons freshly chopped basil, divided use

½ teaspoon dried oregano leaves, divided use

3 ounces slices provolone cheese

1 cup shredded part-skim mozzarella cheese

Tomato sauce for dipping

MAKES 12 APPETIZER-SIZE SLICES

JOHN YARUSI, THE OWNER OF JOHNNY'S PORK ROLL TRUCK, IS SUCH A PORK ROLL ENTHUSIAST THAT HE HAS A COLLECTION OF TAYLOR PROVISIONS MEMORABILIA HE HAS COLLECTED OVER THE YEARS. ALTHOUGH HE SELLS A VARIETY OF DIFFERENT SANDWICHES OUT OF HIS TRUCK, 80 PERCENT OF THE SANDWICHES SOLD ARE THE "JERSEY BREAKFAST" PORK ROLL, EGG, AND CHEESE CLASSIC.

1. Preheat oven to 375 degrees. Coat a baking pan with cooking spray.

2. Spray a small skillet with cooking spray and briefly brown the pork roll pieces. Remove from heat and set aside.

3. Place the bread dough or pizza dough on the prepared pan and pat into a rectangle about 10 by 15 inches (if using pizza dough, rectangle may be slightly smaller). Spread the pork roll pieces lengthwise down the center of the dough.

4. Sprinkle half of the basil and half of the oregano over the meat. Lay the cheese slices over the meat and sprinkle with the remaining half of the herbs, followed by the mozzarella.

5. Fold long sides of dough over filling and press all the edges to seal. Roll over so sealed side is down on the baking pan.

6. Bake for 20 to 23 minutes or until crust is golden brown.

7. Allow to cool briefly on pan, then remove to cutting board to slice. Serve with tomato sauce on the side for dipping.

VARIATIONS

ADD ¼ CUP FINELY CHOPPED RED PEPPER WITH PORK ROLL PIECES (PRECOOK PEPPER BRIEFLY IN SKILLET IF YOU ARE CONCERNED IT WILL BE TOO CRUNCHY).

USE 1 TEASPOON ITALIAN SEASONING IN PLACE OF BASIL AND OREGANO.

SPREAD ¼ CUP TOMATO SAUCE ON DOUGH BEFORE ADDING FILLING INGREDIENTS.

HAWAIIAN PORK ROLL PIZZA

The sweetness of pineapple contrasts nicely with the meaty pork roll and the tang of tomato sauce for an easy lunch dish. Pair it with a salad and you have a simple supper.

1 can refrigerated pizza crust //// Cooking spray	1½ cups cubed pork roll //// 8-ounce can pizza sauce	1¾ cups mozzarella cheese, shredded //// ½ cup canned pineapple chunks, drained

SERVES 2 TO 3

1. Preheat oven to 400 degrees. Unroll dough on ungreased dark nonstick cookie sheet. Press into a 15x10-inch rectangle. Be careful to not overwork the crust.

2. Spray small skillet with cooking spray. Chop pork roll into medium dice and cook until lightly browned. Set aside.

3. Bake dough for about 8 minutes or until lightly golden brown. Top with pizza sauce, half of the cheese, pork roll, and pineapple and finish with the rest of the cheese.

4. Bake 10 minutes longer or until crust is golden brown and cheese is melted. Cool 5 minutes before cutting and serving.

VARIATION

CUT A SWEET RED PEPPER INTO A MEDIUM DICE, MICROWAVE FOR 1 MINUTE TO SOFTEN, AND ADD WITH STEP 3.

PORK ROLL AND RED PEPPER QUICHE

Have we mentioned that pork roll goes well with eggs?

9-inch pie shell, prebaked if desired

////

1 cup pork roll, coarsely chopped

////

¼ cup red pepper, chopped fine

¾ cup shredded cheddar cheese

////

4 eggs

////

1½ cups light cream

¼ teaspoon salt, or to taste

////

¼ teaspoon pepper, or taste

////

¼ teaspoon nutmeg, or seasoning of your choice

MAKES 6 SERVINGS

PORK ROLL HAS A JINGLE, PROCLAIMING, "CASE'S IS THE BEST" AND "SEE WHAT THEY'VE BEEN MISSING WAY OUT WEST."

USE GRATED MOZZARELLA IN PLACE OF CHEDDAR CHEESE.

SUBSTITUTE 1 CUP FROZEN SPINACH, DEFROSTED AND SQUEEZED DRY, IN PLACE OF RED PEPPER.

SAUTÉ 1 TABLESPOON FINELY CHOPPED ONION WITH PORK ROLL.

1. If you are concerned about a soggy crust, pre-bake pie crust according to recipe or package directions. If you have pie weights, use them to keep the crust from puffing up.

2. In small skillet, briefly brown pork roll pieces and soften diced red pepper. Spread filling ingredients in pie shell.

3. Lightly beat eggs, then combine with cheese, cream, salt, pepper, and nutmeg.

4. Carefully pour egg mixture over the filling ingredients.

5. Bake in a preheated 350-degree oven for 35 to 40 minutes or until a knife inserted near the center comes out clean. Let stand for 5 to 10 minutes before cutting into wedges to serve.

BUTTERNUT SQUASH SOUP WITH PORK ROLL

Bites of diced pork roll give this autumn favorite an extra dash of flavor in this recipe from Will Mooney, executive chef and owner of the Brothers Moon Restaurant in Hopewell, New Jersey.

2 butternut squash, peeled and de-seeded

2 cups diced pork roll

1½ cups Spanish onion, chopped small

1 cup celery, chopped small

1 tablespoon chopped garlic

1 bay leaf

1 stick cinnamon

1 pinch nutmeg

1½ quarts vegetable stock

1 tablespoon salt

1 teaspoon fresh ground pepper

SERVES 6 TO 8

1. Roast peeled/de-seeded butternut squash at 300 degrees until soft.

2. Sauté pork roll and then remove pork roll from pot, reserve the meat for later, keep fat in the pot and add onion, celery, and garlic; cook until softened.

3. Add roasted flesh (seeds and skin removed) from butternut squash.

4. Add spices and vegetable stock at this point. Allow to simmer for 20 minutes.

5. When all ingredients are soft, remove cinnamon stick, puree, and adjust seasoning with salt and pepper.

6. Add back the sautéed pork roll, adjust seasoning to your liking and serve.

VARIATION

GARNISH THE SOUP WITH FRESHLY CHOPPED SAGE AND A SPOONFUL OF BROWNED BUTTER.

PORK ROLL DOESN'T CONTAIN ANY GLUTEN.

BLACK BEAN AND PORK ROLL QUESADILLA

This Southwestern favorite gets a pork roll update in this recipe from Will Mooney, executive chef and owner of the Brothers Moon Restaurant in Hopewell, New Jersey.

1½ cups diced pork roll

2 cups cooked black beans

½ red onion, diced small

1 green pepper, seeded and diced small

1 tablespoon chopped garlic

½ cup shredded Monterey Jack cheese

1 teaspoon pepper

2 tortillas (8 to 9 inches)

4 ripe plum tomatoes, halved

4 sprigs cilantro

Salad greens

Sour cream

SERVES 4

FOR A SPICIER VERSION, REMOVE SEEDS (WEAR GLOVES FOR THIS) FROM A SMALL JALAPENO PEPPER AND CHOP FINE. ADD IN STEP 1 WITH THE GREEN PEPPER.

1. Sauté pork roll in a medium hot pan and then add beans, onion, green pepper, garlic, cheese, and pepper, heat through, mixing well and smashing beans slightly.

2. Fill tortillas and place on a greased sheet pan.

3. Season tomatoes with salt and pepper; place on the sheet pan and bake all at 350 degrees for 12 minutes.

4. Serve two tomato halves on a plate with half of a quesadilla. Serve with salad greens and sour cream.

CHARRED ROMAINE, PORK ROLL LARDONS, ROASTED APPLES AND FETA

This flavorful salad is the creation of Kevin Nagle, executive chef of the Cock 'n Bull Restaurant in Peddler's Village, Lahaska, Pennsylvania.

4 Gala apples, unpeeled, with cores removed, quartered

1 tablespoon freshly squeezed lemon juice

2 tablespoons unsalted butter

½ cup vegetable oil

1½ cups of brandy

1 pound pork roll cut into 1-inch dice

3 tablespoons sherry vinegar

2 tablespoons plus 1 teaspoon Dijon mustard

1 tablespoon honey

2 tablespoons water

1 tablespoon olive oil

Kosher salt and fresh ground pepper to taste

4 heads romaine, halved lengthwise and, rinsed, and patted dry

⅓ cup crumbled feta cheese

SERVES 4 TO 6

1. Preheat oven to 350 degrees. Place apple quarters in mixing bowl and add lemon juice, melted butter, vegetable oil, and brandy. Toss apples in mixture until evenly coated.

2. Place apple slices on nonstick baking pan drizzle with remaining liquid and bake uncovered for 20 minutes. Turn apples and continue to cook 6 to 8 more minutes until apples are golden. Take out of oven and let cool to room temperature.

3. Heat 3 tablespoons vegetable oil over medium high heat and cook diced pork roll until crispy but not burnt. Remove from pan and set aside.

4. In a small mixing bowl whisk sherry vinegar, Dijon mustard, honey, water, olive oil, and salt and pepper to taste. Chill in refrigerator.

5. Heat gas grill or a cast-iron grill pan to medium heat. Place romaine halves cut-side down on grill and cook, turning once until charred and slightly wilted, about 4 minutes.

6. Transfer lettuce cut-side up to serving platter season with salt and pepper to taste. Sprinkle pork roll lardons, feta cheese, and roasted apples over romaine and drizzle with dressing.

PORK ROLL AND APPLE FLATBREAD

Bill Murphy, executive chef at Earl's Bucks County in Peddler's Village, Lahaska, Pennsylvania, bakes a different kind of flatbread every day. He shares this one, which combines the sweetness of fall apples with the saltiness of pork roll.

1 recipe flatbread dough, rolled out

////

Dusting of cornmeal

////

¼ cup Honey Crisp apples, peeled and diced to ½ inch by ½ inch

¼ cup Spanish onion, peeled, slices and sautéed

////

¼ cup pork roll, diced ½ inch by ½ inch

¼ cup brie cheese, diced ½ inch by ½ inch

////

Pinch of kosher salt

////

Pinch of black pepper

MAKES 5 SERVINGS

VARIATIONS

SUBSTITUTE CHOPPED PEAR FOR APPLE.

SUBSTITUTE CHEESE OF YOUR CHOICE FOR BRIE.

DUST THE PIZZA PADDLE WITH FLOUR IF YOU DON'T HAVE CORNMEAL.

1. Preheat a pizza stone in a 500-degree oven.

2. Place dough on a cornmeal-treated pizza paddle.

3. Cover dough evenly with apple, onion, and pork roll.

4. Place brie pieces evenly over other ingredients.

5. Dust flatbread with pinches of salt and pepper.

6. Bake on stone until edges are golden brown, spinning around halfway through the process. Cut into five pieces and serve family style.

PORK ROLL ON WONTONS WITH PEACHES AND WHITE CHOCOLATE SAUCE

Sometimes the craziest combinations actually work.

FOR THE WHITE CHOCOLATE SAUCE:

¾ cup water

5 ounces sugar

¼ cup corn syrup

9 ounces white chocolate

FOR THE PORK ROLL ON WONTONS WITH PEACHES:

18 each square wontons

1 tablespoon canola oil

9 slices pork roll

4 cups peaches, peeled, pitted and chopped

1 cup granulated sugar

2 cups whipped cream

SERVES 6 TO 8

1. Preheat oven to 325 degrees for the wontons.

2. To make the white chocolate sauce, heat water, sugar, and corn syrup. Pour over white chocolate. Stir until it comes together. You should have about 1 pint of white chocolate sauce.

3. Brush wontons with canola oil and dust with a little sugar. Bake until golden brown, then allow cooling.

4. Place pork roll slices in hot frying pan for just 1 minute on each side to warm, render out some of the fat and add some color to the slices.

5. Mix chopped peaches with sugar. Assemble, layering the chopped peaches, pork roll, wontons, and whipped cream.

6. Drizzle with white chocolate sauce, and serve.

IF YOU DON'T USE ALL THE WHITE CHOCOLATE SAUCE, IT CAN BE STORED IN THE REFRIGERATOR FOR A FEW WEEKS.

BREAKFAST
AND BRUNCH
BREAKFAST
AND BRUNCH
BREAKFAST
AND BRUNCH
BREAKFAST
AND BRUNCH

BREAKFAST
AND BRUNCH
BREAKFAST
AND BRUNCH
BREAKFAST
AND BRUNCH
BREAKFAST
AND BRUNCH

PORK ROLL SANDWICH

1 soft sandwich roll

1 slice cheese of your choice

2 slices pork roll

Cooking spray

1 egg, cooked to your preference

MAKES 1 SERVING

PORK ROLL IS KNOWN BY SEVERAL NICKNAMES ASSOCIATED WITH THE SLITS OFTEN CUT IN THE MEAT AS IT IS GRILLED TO ALLOW IT TO COOK EVENLY ON THE FLAT TOP INSTEAD OF BUBBLING UP. THE NAMES INCLUDE "PAC MAN BACON" "NOTCH MEAT" OR "FIREMAN'S BADGES" WHEN FOUR SLITS ARE CUT.

Just about every casual restaurant that serves breakfast in New Jersey and Eastern Pennsylvania lists a pork roll sandwich on its menu. It might be a breakfast sandwich with pork roll, egg and cheese, or as a lunch offering with just pork roll and cheese.

1. Toast sandwich roll, if desired, add a slice of cheese and set aside.

2. Lightly spray a medium skillet and add pork roll slices. Don't forget to make small cuts around the edge of pork roll slices so they don't curl during cooking. Cook over medium heat until nicely browned.

3. Meanwhile, on the other side of the skillet, crack an egg and cook it the way you like—scrambled, over easy, or sunny-side up.

4. When the meat and egg are cooked, add them to the sandwich roll. Add mustard or ketchup if you like.

ADD A SLICE OF TOMATO AND A LETTUCE LEAF WITH THE CHEESE IN STEP 1.

PEEL AN ONION AND ADD A FEW THIN SLICES TO THE SKILLET ALONG WITH A TEASPOON OF BUTTER TO COOK ALONGSIDE THE EGG AND PORK ROLL.

SERVE ON AN ENGLISH MUFFIN INSTEAD OF A SANDWICH ROLL.

PORK ROLL HASH WITH FRIED EGG & CHIPOTLE AIOLI

This upscale version of a downhome favorite was created by Kevin Nagle, executive chef at the Cock 'n Bull restaurant in Peddler's Village, Lahaska, Pennsylvania.

FOR THE HASH:

6 Russet potatoes

1 pound Applewood-smoked bacon

2 pounds diced pork roll

1 medium Vidalia (sweet) onion, small dice

½ Fresno pepper, seeds removed and cut to small dice

½ yellow bell pepper, seeds removed and cut to small dice

1 clove garlic, smashed and minced

1 teaspoon smoked paprika

1 teaspoon toasted cumin

2 large eggs

Cilantro for garnish

FOR THE AIOLI:

2 large egg yolks

2 teaspoons fresh lemon juice

½ teaspoon Dijon mustard

¼ cup extra-virgin olive oil

3 tablespoons canola oil

2 garlic cloves, smashed and minced

1 canned chipotle pepper, seeds removed

2 ounces adobo sauce

MAKES 1 SERVING

1. Dice Russet potatoes, leaving skin on, and blanch in boiling water with two tablespoons kosher salt for 15 minutes. Drain potatoes and pat dry.

2. Heat large sauté pan over medium heat and add diced bacon and pork roll. Cook until bacon is crisp but not burnt.

3. Remove bacon and pork roll and add potatoes, onions, peppers, and garlic and cook over medium heat for 15 minutes or until onions are translucent. Add paprika and cumin and cook for an additional 10 minutes and remove from heat.

4. In a bowl combine egg yolks, lemon juice, and mustard whisk until incorporated. Combine oils and add a few drops at a time to egg mixture, whisking constantly, until all oil is incorporated and mixture is emulsified. Whisk in garlic paste and chopped chipotle pepper and adobo sauce. If mixture is too thick, thin with a few drops of water. Transfer mixture to squeeze bottle and set aside.

5. In medium nonstick pan, fry two eggs for 3 minutes on each side. Move hash to a large plate, placing eggs carefully on top without breaking yolks. Using a squeeze bottle, stripe the egg-and-hash mixture with aioli and garnish with chopped fresh cilantro.

SEVERAL COMPANIES SHIP PORK ROLL OUT TO DIFFERENT AREAS OF THE COUNTRY AND EVEN WORLDWIDE TO SATISFY THE LONGING DESIRE OF EX-PATS SALIVATING FOR PORK ROLL THAT CAN'T BE FOUND AT THEIR GROCERY STORE.

CRISPY PORK ROLL HASH

Traditionally hash is a combination of corned, spices, and potatoes, but you don't need corned beef to make this breakfast favorite that also works as a lunch dish or a light supper.

2 to 3 cups chopped cooked potatoes, Russet or Yukon gold	1 medium onion, peeled and finely chopped (about 1 cup)	Salt and pepper to taste
2 to 3 tablespoons unsalted butter	2 to 3 cups coarsely chopped pork roll	Chopped fresh parsley for garnish (optional)

MAKES 4 TO 6 SERVINGS

IN THE CHILDREN'S PICTURE BOOK "I LOVE PORK ROLL," AUTHOR BRUCE LARKIN IS DEPICTED MAKING A SANDWICH.

TOP WITH A FRIED EGG FOR ADDED FLAVOR AND PROTEIN.

·············

ADD ¼ CUP FINELY CHOPPED SWEET PEPPER OR TOMATO OR A CHOPPED CLOVE OF GARLIC TO SKILLET WHEN COOKING ONION.

·············

1. Peel and chop potatoes to a ½-inch dice. If you don't have leftovers and are using raw potatoes, cook chopped potatoes at a medium boil for about 3 minutes, until just tender. Drain and set aside.

2. Heat butter in a large skillet over medium heat. Add the onion and cook a few minutes, until fragrant and translucent.

3. Add the chopped pork roll and potatoes. Spread evenly in the pan. Increase the heat to high or medium high and press down on the mixture with a spatula.

4. Do not stir the mixture; allow it to brown. When nicely browned on the bottom, flip it over, press down on it again and allow to brown on the other side. Don't allow it to stick; add more butter if necessary.

5. Remove from heat and add salt and pepper to taste. Sprinkle with parsley, if using.

CHEESY PORK ROLL MUFFINS

These savory muffins are almost a meal by themselves but also are a great addition to any brunch gathering. Freeze some individually to take out and defrost for a quick, on-the-go breakfast.

12 slices pork roll

////

Cooking spray, if using

////

4 cups all-purpose flour

2 cups shredded Cheddar cheese

////

2 tablespoons baking powder

////

½ teaspoon ground black pepper

2 eggs

////

½ cup vegetable oil

2 cups milk

MAKES 2 DOZEN MUFFINS

1. Chop pork roll into small cubes and cook in a skillet over medium-high heat until lightly browned. Set aside on paper towels to drain.

2. Preheat oven to 400 degrees. Coat 24 muffin cups with cooking spray or insert cupcake papers in each.

3. Mix flour, Cheddar cheese, baking powder, and black pepper in a large medium bowl.

4. Beat eggs, milk, and vegetable oil together in a small bowl; stir into flour mixture until just moistened. Gently fold pork roll pieces into batter. Spoon batter into the prepared muffin cups.

5. Bake in the preheated oven until a toothpick inserted into the center comes out clean, 15 to 20 minutes. Serve warm.

VARIATION

DRAIN AND CHOP A 4-OUNCE CAN OF CHILES AND ADD TO BATTER IN STEP 4 WITH PORK ROLL.

WHILE PORK ROLL HAS BEEN CALLED THE COUSIN OF BOLOGNA OR COMPARED TO CANADIAN BACON, THE MEAT IS DISTINCT WITH A SALTY, MOUTHWATERING AND MEATY FLAVOR.

STUFFED FRENCH TOAST

French toast was never like this before. Cheese and pork roll add flavor and texture to this popular breakfast entrée. A drizzle of maple syrup creates an enticing salty-sweet combination.

Cooking spray

6 slices pork roll

1 loaf French bread, cut into a dozen ½-inch-thick slices

½ teaspoon butter

6 slices cheddar cheese

6 eggs, slightly beaten

2 cups milk

1 teaspoon Dijon mustard

Maple syrup for serving

MAKES 6 SERVINGS

1. The night before, or 6 hours before serving, spray medium skillet with cooking spray and briefly brown pork roll slices after making small cuts around the edges to prevent the pork roll from curling.

2. Butter an 11-by-7-inch baking dish and place 6 slices French bread in a single layer on the bottom. Top each slice of bread with a slice of pork roll and a slice of cheese. Top each with remaining slices of French bread.

3. In medium bowl, whisk together eggs, milk, and Dijon mustard. Pour mixture slowly over bread layers in baking dish. Cover and refrigerate 6 hours or overnight.

4. Remove from refrigerator a half-hour before baking. Preheat oven to 350 degrees. Bake, uncovered, 50 to 55 minutes or until golden brown and knife inserted in center comes out clean.

VARIATIONS

DRAIN AND CHOP A 4-OUNCE CAN OF CHILES AND ADD TO EGG MIXTURE BEFORE POURING OVER BREAD

....

FOR A SPICY VERSION, ADD ½ TEASPOON TO 1 TEASPOON DRIED CRUSHED RED PEPPER.

....

MILD PORK ROLL SELLS BETTER IN NORTHERN NEW JERSEY, WHILE TANGY PORK ROLL IS MORE POPULAR IN SOUTHERN NEW JERSEY.

PORK ROLL STRATA

This is a nice entrée for a group breakfast or brunch that you put together the night before, then bake just before serving.

2 medium onions, peeled and sliced

////

¾ cup each sweet red and green pepper, diced small

////

1 teaspoon olive oil

1 loaf French bread, cut into small cubes

////

1½ cups diced pork roll

////

1 cup shredded Monterey Jack cheese

6 eggs

////

2 cups milk

////

Salt and pepper to taste

MAKES 6 TO 8 SERVINGS

LEN BOCCASSINI, A FOOD WRITER AND BLOGGER AT FOODIDUDE, SAID HE HAS SUCH A LOVE FOR PORK ROLL THAT HE ALWAYS MAKES SURE TO INTRODUCE HIS FOODIE FRIENDS WHO WORK IN THE CULINARY INDUSTRY TO THE PRODUCT WHEN THEY PASS THROUGH TOWN ON A VISIT. EVEN THE MOST HIGHBROW FOODIE ENJOYS A JERSEY BREAKFAST.

1. Grease a 13-by-9-inch baking pan.

2. Using a large skillet, sauté onions and peppers in oil.

3. Spread half of the bread cubes in the greased baking pan and sprinkle with half of the pepper-and-onion mixture, chopped pork roll and cheese. Repeat layers.

4. In a bowl, beat the eggs, milk, salt, and pepper. Pour egg mixture over bread layers, cover and refrigerate overnight.

5. Remove the strata from the refrigerator 30 minutes before baking and uncover. Preheat oven to 350 degrees. Bake uncovered for 30 to 35 minutes or until a knife inserted in the center comes out clean.

VARIATIONS

ADD A PEELED, MINCED CLOVE OF GARLIC IN STEP 2.

. . . .

USE CHEDDAR OR PROVOLONE CHEESE INSTEAD OF THE MONTEREY JACK.

. . . .

POTATO PANCAKES WITH CHEESE AND PORK ROLL

The next time you make mashed potatoes for dinner, cook extra so you have leftovers to make this easy, flavorful breakfast dish.

Cooking spray

½ cup pork roll, diced small

3 cups chilled mashed potatoes

⅔ cup grated cheddar cheese

2 tablespoons sweet onion, peeled and chopped fine

1 to 2 eggs, lightly beaten

3 tablespoons plus ½ cup all-purpose flour

Vegetable oil for frying

Kosher salt

Sour cream (optional)

MAKES A DOZEN PANCAKES

1. Spray small skillet with cooking spray and brown pork roll pieces briefly. Remove to paper towel to drain.

2. In a large bowl, stir together the mashed potatoes, pork roll, cheese, onions, egg (use two if the potatoes seem dry), and 3 tablespoons flour. Using about 1/4 cup of the mixture for each, roll 12 balls, then flatten into pancakes about a half-inch thick.

3. Place the remaining 1/2 cup flour in a shallow dish and coat each pancake in the flour. Work carefully as the pancakes can fall apart.

4. Heat 3 to 4 tablespoons of vegetable oil in a large skillet over medium heat.

5. Fry the pancakes, in batches, for 3 to 4 minutes on each side, being careful to not flip them over until they are golden brown and crispy. Add more oil to the pan as needed between batches. Transfer the pancakes to a plate lined with paper towels and immediately sprinkle them with kosher salt, to taste.

6. Serve the potato pancakes topped with sour cream, if desired.

"TOP CHEF" ALUM AND NEW JERSEY NATIVE MIKE ISABELLA MAKES HIS OWN PORK ROLL AT HIS RESTAURANTS IN WASHINGTON, D.C. "IT IS NOT HARD TO MAKE," HE SAID. "IT IS TASTY AND IT FITS THE STYLE OF COOKING WE DO."

EGGS SCRAMBLED WITH PORK ROLL AND POTATOES

Your eggs, pork roll, and potatoes come all in one dish is this easy breakfast meal.

2 tablespoons olive oil

2 large potatoes, peeled and diced

1 cup pork roll, coarsely chopped into bite-sized pieces

½ medium onion, peeled and cut to a small dice

Dash of freshly ground pepper

4 to 6 large eggs

Pinch of salt

MAKES 4 SERVINGS

VARIATION

ADD 1 TEASPOON FINELY CHOPPED FRESH ROSEMARY OR ⅛ TEASPOON DRIED ROSEMARY WITH PEPPER IN STEP 1.

1. Heat the oil in a large skillet over medium high heat and sauté potatoes for about 10 minutes, stirring frequently. Add the chopped pork roll and onion and cook until the onion is tender. Remove from heat. Stir in the pepper.

2. Whisk the egg with the salt in a medium-sized bowl. Reduce the heat to low and return the skillet to the heat. Pour the eggs over the pork roll mixture and cook, stirring gently until the eggs are set. Serve immediately.

CHEESY PORK ROLL OMELET

This easy omelet is finished in the oven, and pieces of chopped pork roll give add a little something extra to the flavor.

1 tablespoon butter	1 medium potato, cooked, peeled and diced	½ cup diced pork roll
4 eggs		2 garlic cloves, peeled and minced
⅔ cup cheddar cheese, divided use	¼ cup diced onion	

MAKES 2 SERVINGS

1. Preheat oven to 450 degrees.

2. Melt butter over medium heat in an ovenproof skillet. In small bowl, combine eggs and ⅓ cup of the cheese.

3. Combine potato, onion, pork roll, and garlic in skillet. Cook over medium heat for 5 minutes, until onion is translucent. Stir in egg mixture and make sure it spreads evenly over bottom of skillet. Cook over medium heat for 5 minutes or until almost set.

4. Place skillet in preheated 450-degree oven and bake for 5 minutes. Remove from oven, sprinkle with remaining cheese, then return to oven and bake until cheese melts.

5. Cut into wedges and serve warm.

FOR YEARS TAYLOR PROVISIONS AND CASE'S PORK ROLL HAVE BEEN TRYING TO DIVERSIFY THE WAY NEW JERSEYANS EAT THE STATE'S SIGNATURE MEAT, PUTTING OUT RECIPE BOOKS AND ADVERTISING PORK ROLL BAKED AND SERVED WITH PINEAPPLE OR REPLACING A HAM IN OTHER DINNER-TIME MEALS.

PORK ROLL AND CHEESE CREPES

PORK ROLL AND CHEESE CREPES

The elegant crepe gets a downhome makeover with pork roll in this recipe. Ready-to-fill crepes are available in supermarkets, but just in case you want to make your own, we included the directions.

FOR THE FILLING:

Cooking spray

2 cups pork roll, chopped to ½ inch by ½ inch

½ cup onion, finely chopped

8 slices cheddar cheese

Sour cream (optional)

FOR THE CREPES:

1 cup all-purpose flour

2 large eggs

½ cup milk

½ cup water

¼ teaspoon salt

2 tablespoons butter, melted

MAKES 4 SERVINGS

1. Spray a large, nonstick skillet with cooking spray and cook pork roll and onion over medium heat for 3 minutes or until meat is browned and onions are softened. Set aside.

2. To prepare crepes, whisk the flour and eggs in a large mixing bowl. Gradually add the milk and water, stirring to combine. Add the salt and butter; beat until smooth.

3. Heat a lightly oiled griddle or small frying pan over medium-high heat.

4. Pour ¼ cup batter for each crepe onto the griddle or into the frying pan. If using a pan, tilt lightly to swirl the batter so it coats the surface evenly.

5. Cook the crepe for about 2 minutes, until the bottom is lightly browned. Loosen with a spatula, turn and cook the other side. After each crepe cooks, set it aside on a platter.

6. Once all the crepes are cooked, plate 2 heaping tablespoons of the pork roll and onion mixture onto each center, add a slice of cheese, fold in the sides and roll up.

7. Place rolled crepes back on hot pan, cook briefly until crisp on each side. Serve with sour cream on the side.

SOUPS AND
SANDWICHES
SOUPS AND
SANDWICHES
SOUPS AND
SANDWICHES
SOUPS AND
SANDWICHES
SOUPS AND
SANDWICHES

SOUPS AND SANDWICHES

SOUPS AND SANDWICHES

SOUPS AND SANDWICHES

SOUPS AND SANDWICHES

SOUPS AND SANDWICHES

PORK ROLL MONTE CRISTO SANDWICH

The Monte Cristo is a variation of the French croque-monsieur, a grilled ham and cheese sandwich. This variation is shared by Will Mooney, executive chef and owner of the Brothers Moon Restaurant in Hopewell, New Jersey.

12 slices pork roll	6 slices Muenster cheese, cut in half	¼ cup milk
12 slices white bread	2 large eggs	3 tablespoons butter

MAKES 6 SANDWICHES

1. Cook pork roll slices until golden brown.

2. Layer cheese and pork roll on 6 slices bread; cover with remaining slices bread.

3. In bowl, mix eggs and milk; quickly dip both sides of sandwiches into egg mixture.

4. On griddle or in skillet, sauté sandwiches in butter over medium heat until cheese is melted and both sides are browned.

IN LOS ANGELES'S KOREA-TOWN SECTION, WHIZ, A CHEESESTEAK AND SANDWICH SHOP SERVES UP PORK ROLL, EGG, AND CHEESE SANDWICHES ALONGSIDE AUTHENTIC PHILLY CHEESESTEAKS.

EGG SALAD WITH PORK ROLL

With this recipe you can perk up traditional egg salad with small bites of lightly browned pork roll.

6 hard-cooked eggs, peeled and chopped fine

////

Cooking spray

////

1 cup pork roll, cut to small dice

2 tablespoons regular or light mayonnaise, creamy salad dressing, or plain yogurt

////

¼ cup onion, peeled and chopped (optional)

2 teaspoons Dijon mustard, or to taste

////

Salt and pepper to taste

ENOUGH FOR 4 SANDWICHES OR SALAD PLATES

IN DAYS GONE BY, PORK ROLL WAS SOLD IN NEW JERSEY DELIS AND SLICED FRESH LIKE LUNCHMEAT THAT YOU PURCHASE TODAY.

1. Hard-boil the eggs, remove from stove, and cover with cold water.

2. Cook pork roll pieces in skillet lightly sprayed with cooking spray. Remove to paper towel to drain.

3. Peel and coarsely chop eggs and combine with mayonnaise, onion, mustard, pork roll, salt, and pepper until well blended.

4. Use as a filling for sandwiches, a topping for crackers or on a salad plate with scoops of tuna salad, a few leaves of lettuce, and sliced tomatoes.

VARIATIONS

USE HONEY DIJON OR STONEGROUND MUSTARD IN PLACE OF DIJON.

DRAIN AND CHOP A 4-OUNCE CAN OF CHILES AND ADD WITH OTHER INGREDIENTS IN STEP 3.

DRAIN AND CHOP 1 TABLESPOON OF GREEN OLIVES AND ADD WITH OTHER INGREDIENTS IN STEP 3.

TOMATO VEGETABLE SOUP WITH PORK ROLL

This hearty soup is perfect for a chilly day with plenty of vegetables and meaty pork roll.

1 large can of peeled Italian-style whole plum tomatoes

2 cups of coarsely chopped pork roll

1 medium onion, peeled and chopped

1½ cups sweet corn

2 potatoes, peeled and cut into a one-inch dice

2 carrots, sliced into thin rounds

1 rib celery, chopped fine

1 tablespoon soy sauce

1 teaspoon salt

1 teaspoon pepper sauce (optional)

3 cups of chicken or vegetable broth

MAKES 8 SERVINGS

1. Roughly chop the tomatoes.

2. Combine all ingredients, including juice from tomatoes, in a large soup pot and cook on simmer until the potatoes and carrots are tender, about 35 to 40 minutes. Serve with slices of whole grain bread.

VARIATION

SERVE WITH A SMALL BOWL OF SOUR CREAM SO YOUR GUESTS CAN ADD A DOLLOP IF THEY WANT

POTATO PORK ROLL SOUP

Pork roll and potatoes; can it get any better than this? This creamy soup is a warm and satisfying winter meal.

4 to 5 large potatoes, peeled and cut into 1-inch cubes	1½ cups pork roll, cut to ½-inch dice	3 cups milk
1 medium onion, peeled and chopped fine	3 tablespoons butter	8 ounces heavy cream
4 celery stalks, chopped fine	3 tablespoons all-purpose flour	8 ounces sour cream
		Salt and pepper to taste

MAKES 10 SERVINGS

1. Combine potatoes, onions, celery, and pork roll in a large saucepan. Add just enough water to cover. Cook on high until potatoes and celery are fork-tender.

2. Meanwhile, in a small saucepan melt butter, add flour and whisk together until combined to create a roux. Stir in milk and whisk until it just begins to thicken.

3. Stir whipping cream and sour cream into white sauce.

4. Add white sauce and pork roll to potato, veggie, and water mixture. Stir to combine and allow to warm briefly on stove, about 2 minutes.

5. Season to taste with salt and pepper and serve.

ASIDE FROM THE DEBATE OVER WHAT TO CALL THE SWEET MEAT, OTHERS DEBATE WHICH BREAD IS BEST. FOR THIS UNUSUAL SANDWICH, WE RECOMMEND A PRETZEL ROLL.

PORK ROLL AND PEANUT BUTTER SANDWICH

Chef Sean Browne at Buttonwood Grill in Peddler's Village, Lahaska, Pennsylvania, created this sandwich, which gives a whole new meaning to grilled cheese.

3 slices of pork roll //// Pretzel roll (or bread of your choice)	3 ounces chunky peanut butter	¼ Granny Smith apple, sliced thin //// 2 ounces cream cheese

MAKES 1 SANDWICH

1. On a hot griddle, cook pork roll on each side until browned.

2. While the pork roll is browning, toast bread and liberally spread peanut butter on bottom piece and lay thinly sliced apples on top. Spread cream cheese on other piece of bread.

3. When pork roll is cooked, place on top of sliced apples and close sandwich.

MAIN MEALS

MAIN MEALS

MAIN MEALS

MAIN MEALS

MAIN MEALS

MAIN MEALS

MAIN MEALS

MAIN MEALS

MAIN MEALS

TRENTON-STYLE SPAGHETTI A LA CARBONARA

Randy Forrester, chef de cuisine at the Brothers Moon Restaurant in Hopewell, New Jersey, created this Jersey-style version of a traditional Italian favorite.

1 pound spaghetti

4 large egg yolks

1 cup freshly grated Parmesan cheese (3 ounces), plus more for serving

1 tablespoon extra-virgin olive oil

6 ounces pork roll, frozen and then grated, or cut into ⅛-inch dice

2 garlic cloves, thinly sliced

Pinch of freshly grated nutmeg

Freshly ground pepper

SERVES 4 TO 6

1. In a large pot of boiling salted water, cook the spaghetti until just al dente. Drain, reserving ½ cup of the pasta cooking water.

2. Meanwhile, in a small bowl, whisk the egg yolks, cheese, and reserved cooking water.

3. In a large, deep skillet, heat the oil. Add half of the pork roll and cook over moderately high heat, stirring, until crisp, 4 minutes. Add the garlic and cook until golden, 1 minute.

4. Add the hot spaghetti to the skillet. Pull the skillet off the heat, tossing, until coated. Slowly add the reserved pasta cooking water, beaten egg yolks, and cheese. Toss until coated with a creamy sauce, about 1 minute. Add nutmeg, and season with pepper.

5. Transfer to bowls, top with the remaining grated pork roll and serve, passing extra Parmesan.

EASY PORK ROLL MEATLOAF

Even Mom would like this update of her favorite meatloaf that uses pork roll to add moisture and flavor to a popular, homespun favorite. Serve with mashed potatoes and your favorite vegetable.

FOR THE MEATLOAF:

1 pound 85 percent lean ground beef

½ pound pork roll, ground or chopped fine

½ cup quick-cooking oatmeal

½ cup milk

¼ cup chopped onion

1 large egg, lightly beaten

½ teaspoon salt

¼ teaspoon pepper

Cooking spray

FOR THE TOPPING:

⅓ cup ketchup

2 tablespoons brown sugar

1 tablespoon yellow mustard

SERVES 4 TO 6

1. Combine meats, oatmeal, milk, onion, and egg in a large bowl and mix until blended. Lightly spray a 9x5-inch loaf pan or a 9x13-inch pan with cooking spray. Place mixture in prepared pan; if using the larger pan, mold mixture into a loaf shape and place in center.

2. Stir together ketchup, brown sugar, and yellow mustard and pour evenly over meatloaf.

3. Bake at 350 degrees for 1 hour. Remove from oven and let stand 5 minutes. Remove loaf from pan before slicing to serve.

VARIATIONS

SUBSTITUTE ½ CUP SEASONED BREAD CRUMBS FOR OATMEAL AND OMIT SALT AND PEPPER. ITALIAN SEASONED BREAD CRUMBS WORK WELL IN THIS RECIPE.

FOR A SPICY VERSION, ADD 2 TABLESPOONS EACH CHOPPED JALAPENO PEPPERS AND ROASTED RED PEPPERS.

PORK ROLL SCALLOPED POTATOES

Scalloped potatoes are easier to make than many home cooks realize, and this version, fortified with pork roll, would make an ideal dish for a potluck dinner, tailgating party, or family gathering.

1 cup pork roll, cut into small cubes

Cooking spray

6 to 8 cups potatoes, peeled and thinly sliced

6 to 8 scallions (the white part), diced

½ teaspoon salt

Freshly ground black pepper to taste

6 to 8 tablespoons butter, cut into pieces

1¾ cups light cream or half-and-half

MAKES 6 TO 8 SERVINGS

NEW JERSEY IS KNOWN AS THE DINER CAPITAL OF THE WORLD, AND PORK ROLL OR TAYLOR HAM IS SERVED IN MOST DINERS IN THE STATE.

1. Dice pork roll and cook briefly in small skillet lightly coated with cooking spray. Set aside.

2. Preheat oven to 350 degrees and grease a 9x13-inch pan or a two-quart casserole dish.

3. Alternate layers of potatoes, scallions, and pork roll, lightly salting and peppering each layer. Dot each layer with pieces of butter.

4. Warm the cream or half-and-half briefly and pour over the potato mixture. Bake, uncovered, for 1 hour, until the top is lightly browned the potatoes are tender.

PORKROLLNITA

This recipe comes from T.C. Nelson, owner of Trenton Social in Trenton, New Jersey, where the first Pork Roll Festival was held. He served this dish at the festival and reports that it sold out quickly. Its name is a take-off on the Spanish carnita.

FOR THE PORK SHOULDER:

A 1-pound pork butt shoulder

Salt and pepper to taste

Smoked paprika, cayenne pepper, thyme, and fresh garlic to taste

1 can root beer

FOR THE PICO DE GALLO:

2 medium slicing tomatoes or 4 plum tomatoes

1 small onion, peeled and diced

1 tablespoon chopped fresh cilantro

4 green onions (just the white part), chopped

Powdered garlic, salt, and pepper to taste

TO FINISH THE SANDWICHES:

4 slices pork roll

Cooking spray

6 slices Swiss cheese

6 flour tortillas

2 limes, cut into wedges

MAKES 6 SANDWICHES

1. Cook the pork butt should by combining all the seasonings in a small bowl and rubbing evenly over roast. Place meat in a slow cooker. Add root beer and cook on Low for 6 to 8 hours or High for 4 to 5 hours or until pork is very tender. If making ahead, refrigerate the pork and rewarm when ready to make your PorkRollNitas.

2. Prepare the pico de gallo. In a medium bowl, combine tomato, onion, cilantro, and green onion. Season with garlic, salt, and pepper. Stir until evenly distributed. Refrigerate for 30 minutes.

3. Cut pork roll into matchstick-sized julienne strips using a culinary knife. Briefly fry pork roll in cooking spray until pieces begin to brown.

4. Layer each flour tortilla with a slice of Swiss cheese, warm pulled pork, and julienne strips of pork roll, then top with a spoonful of the pico de gallo. Serve with lime wedges for squeezing.

VARIATIONS

USE CHEDDAR OR PROVOLONE CHEESE INSTEAD OF SWISS.

....

DRAIN AND CHOP 3 TABLESPOONS OF ROASTED RED PEPPERS (7-OUNCE JAR) AND ADD BETWEEN MEAT LAYERS.

....

CHEESY PORK ROLL CASSEROLE

One-pot meals are quick and easy, and this one combines all the major food groups plus pork roll for added flavor and texture.

1 ½ cups uncooked pasta of your choice

1 tablespoon olive oil

2 tablespoons onion, chopped small

½ cup red or green pepper, chopped small

2 cups chopped broccoli (thaw if frozen)

½ cup mayonnaise or creamy salad dressing

1 ½ cups (6 ounces) shredded cheddar cheese

1 ½ cups pork roll, cut into small cubes

¼ cup milk

¾ cup seasoned croutons (optional)

MAKES 4 TO 6 SERVINGS.

1. Prepare pasta according to package directions, drain and set aside.

2. Cook onion, pepper and broccoli in olive oil until vegetables begin to soften. Combine all ingredients except cup of the cheese and the croutons, if using.

3. Spoon the mixture into a greased 1 quart casserole and sprinkle with remaining cheese and croutons. Bake at 350 degrees for 30 minutes, until hot and starting to bubble lightly along the sides.

VARIATION

HALVE TWO PLUM TOMATOES AND SQUEEZE OUT THE SEEDS. CHOP FINE AND ADD IN STEP 3.

PORK ROLL MAC AND CHEESE

Macaroni and cheese gets more flavor and an extra blast of protein in this revamped recipe from Will Mooney, executive chef and owner of Brothers Moon Restaurant in Hopewell, New Jersey.

½ pound elbow macaroni

1 tablespoon all-purpose flour

2 tablespoons butter divided

12 ounces diced pork roll

½ cup bread crumbs

1 pinch ground red pepper (cayenne)

2 cups milk

⅛ teaspoon paprika

½ pound cheddar, diced

¼ teaspoon salt

MAKES 4 TO 6 SERVINGS

1. Heat oven to 400 degrees. Lightly grease 2-quart casserole dish.

2. Cook macaroni according to directions; drain.

3. In casserole dish, stir together diced pork roll and elbow macaroni.

4. In medium saucepan, melt 1 tablespoon butter. Blend in flour, salt, black pepper, and cayenne until smooth. Stir in milk; cook over medium heat, stirring, until mixture thickens and boils. Add cheese; cook, stirring, until cheese is melted. Pour over pork roll mixture; mix well.

5. Melt remaining 1 tablespoon butter; stir in bread crumbs and paprika. Sprinkle over macaroni. Bake 20 to 25 minutes.

GLAZED BAKED PORK ROLL

The sweetness of brown sugar contrasts nicely with the saltiness of pork roll for this main dish that will warm the hearts of pork roll fans. For a traditional meal, serve with steamed carrots or green beans and a scoop of mashed potatoes.

1½ pounds pork roll	Cloves	⅓ cup firmly packed brown sugar
////	////	////
1 teaspoon water	1 teaspoon mustard	½ teaspoon vinegar

MAKES 4 SERVINGS

1. Preheat oven to 375 degrees.

2. Place pork roll on rack in a shallow baking pan. Using a sharp knife, lightly score surface and stud with cloves.

3. Combine brown sugar, water, mustard, and vinegar and stir until smooth. Brush glaze over pork roll.

4. Bake 35 minutes or until meat is warm in the center. Baste occasionally while cooking. When ready to serve, slice thin and spoon any remaining glaze over the pork roll after it is moved to a plate.

ROASTED SWEET POTATOES AND PORK ROLL

This combination of sweet potatoes and pork roll tastes like autumn and is a perfect side dish for a hearty meal. In a pinch, it could stand alone as a light supper.

1 tablespoon olive oil //// ½ teaspoon paprika	8 sweet potatoes, scrubbed and sliced lengthwise into quarters (don't peel)	1 cup pork roll, diced

MAKES 8 SERVINGS

1. Preheat oven to 400 degrees. Lightly grease a baking sheet.

2. In a large bowl, mix olive oil and paprika. Add potato sticks and pork roll, and stir gently to coat. Place potato slices on the prepared baking sheet. Pour any remaining oil mixture over slices.

3. Bake 40 minutes in the preheated oven, turning once.

PORK ROLL AND CHEESE BISCUITS

These meaty biscuits are a great companion to a hearty soup. Or serve them alongside scrambled eggs—maybe even with pork scrambled in.

1 cup pork roll, cut to small dice

////

½ cup shredded cheddar cheese

2 cups all-purpose flour

////

5 teaspoons baking powder

////

1 teaspoon salt

2 tablespoons butter or shortening

////

¾ cup cold milk

MAKES 16 BISCUITS

1. Preheat oven to 450 degrees. In a small skillet, briefly cook pork roll until lightly browned. Set aside to cool.

2. Sift the flour, baking powder and salt into a medium-sized mixing bowl. Work the butter into the flour mixture with your fingers or a pastry blender.

3. Gradually add the milk, mixing gently until just blended. Add shredded cheese and pork roll and mix just enough to combine. Don't overwork the dough.

4. Turn dough onto your floured counter and roll lightly to about a half-inch thick. Using a glass or a biscuit cutter, cut out three-inch rounds and place biscuits on a cookie sheet. Bake until lightly browned, about 12 to 15 minutes. Serve immediately.

CORNBREAD AND PORK ROLL CASSEROLE

Cornbread casserole is an easy old-fashioned favorite and a perfect side dish for roast chicken or pork chops. Adding chopped pork roll gives it more flavor and texture.

1 cup pork roll, cut into small cubes

////

1 can (15¼ ounces) whole kernel corn, drained

////

1 can (14¾ ounces) cream-style corn

1 package (8½ ounces) cornbread or corn muffin mix

////

1 egg

////

2 tablespoons butter, melted

¼ teaspoon garlic powder (optional)

////

¼ teaspoon paprika (optional)

MAKES 4 TO 6 SERVINGS

1. Cook pork roll briefly in skillet, just until it starts to brown around the edges. Remove from skillet and drain on paper towel. Allow to cool.

2. Preheat oven to 400 degrees.

3. In a large bowl, combine all ingredients. Pour into a greased, 11x7-inch baking dish. Bake, uncovered, for 25 to 30 minutes or until the top and edges are golden brown.

VARIATION

MIX IN ¼ CUP CHOPPED JALAPENO PEPPERS TO ADD A LITTLE SPICINESS.

PORK ROLL ALFREDO

This creamy, rich Alfredo recipe gets an extra flavor boost from the savory pork roll.

12-ounce box fettuccine

////

½ pound pork roll, diced fine

Cooking spray

////

1 stick butter

////

⅔ cup light cream

½ cup grated Parmesan cheese

////

1 egg yolk, slightly beaten

MAKES 4 SERVINGS

1. Spray small skillet with cooking spray and briefly brown the pork roll. Set aside.

2. Cook pasta according to package directions.

3. While pasta is cooking, melt butter in a medium saucepan. Remove from heat. Gradually stir in the cream, Parmesan cheese, and egg yolk. Pour sauce over hot pasta and toss to coat well. Add cooked pork roll.

VARIATION

AFTER COOKING PORK ROLL, REMOVE FROM PAN AND ADD 1 TEASPOON OLIVE OIL AND COOK FINELY CHOPPED ½ CUP RED PEPPER OR ½ CUP BROCCOLI. ADD VEGETABLES WITH PORK ROLL IN STEP 2.

PORK ROLL FRIED RICE

Pork roll blends easily into this fragrant recipe for fried rice from Bill Murphy, executive chef at Earl's Bucks County in Peddler's Village, Lahaska, Pennsylvania.

1 cup pork roll, diced ½ inch by ½ inch

2 tablespoons garlic, peeled and chopped

2 tablespoons fresh ginger, chopped

2 tablespoons scallion, chopped

2 tablespoons carrot, chopped fine

2 tablespoons Spanish onion, chopped fine

2 tablespoons red pepper, chopped fine

1½ quarts jasmine rice, cooked according to package directions.

2 eggs, cracked and beaten

¼ cup oyster sauce

2 tablespoons soy sauce

2 teaspoons toasted sesame oil

½ tablespoon crushed red pepper flakes

½ cup canola oil

½ cup pineapple, diced ½ inch by ½ inch

MAKES 4 SERVINGS

1. Heat large sauce pot on high heat and add oil. Heat until it shimmers.

2. Add pork roll, sauté for 1 minute or until it begins to brown.

3. Add vegetables and sauté for 2 minutes or until you smell the ginger and garlic essence.

4. Add the rice and cook 1 minute stirring constantly.

5. Add sauces, oils, eggs, and crushed pepper flakes, mixing thoroughly.

6. Add pineapple and heat mixture until pineapple is warm but not mushy. Serve in a large bowl, family style.

EASY PORK ROLL CASSOULET

A little bit French and a little bit Jersey, this meaty casserole is hearty and filling. Serve with Pork Roll and Cheese Biscuits, if you just can't get enough pork roll.

1 pound pork roll, cut into bite-sized chunks

2 tablespoons olive oil

1 medium onion, peeled and chopped

2 garlic cloves, peeled and minced

3 medium carrots, thinly sliced

1 can (16 ounces) kidney beans, rinsed and drained

1 can (15 ounces) black beans, rinsed and drained

1 can (15 ounces) cannellini or other white beans, rinsed and drained

1 can (15 ounces) diced tomatoes with basil, garlic and oregano

½ cup wine of your choice or beef broth

1 bay leaf

MAKES 9 SERVINGS

1. Preheat oven to 375 degrees. Grease a 3-quart baking dish. In a large skillet over medium-high heat, briefly cook the pork roll in the olive oil until lightly browned. Remove from skillet and set aside.

2. Add onion, garlic, and carrots, to skillet. Cook, stirring, about 5 minutes.

3. Combine pork roll, onion mixture, beans, tomatoes, wine or broth, and bay leaf in casserole dish. Stir gently.

3. Cover and bake for 50 minutes and test by poking a carrot slice with a fork. Cassoulet is ready when the carrots are tender. Remove bay leaf before serving.

VARIATIONS

UNCOVER CASSEROLE AND SPRINKLE TOP WITH ½ CUP BUTTERED BREAD CRUMBS FOR LAST 15 MINUTES OF BAKING.

PORK ROLL AND RICE CASSEROLE

This is a filling and flavorful one-pan dish that is perfect to share at a potluck or tailgating party.

2 pounds pork roll, cut into bite-size pieces

1 tablespoon oil

4 celery ribs, thinly sliced

1 large onion, peeled and chopped

1 large green pepper, peeled and chopped

4½ cups water

1 can (10¾ ounces) condensed cream of chicken soup

1 cup uncooked rice

¾ cup of any dried chicken noodle soup mix

¼ cup bread crumbs

2 tablespoons butter, melted

MAKES 12 TO 14 SERVINGS

1. Grease a 13x9-inch baking pan. Preheat oven to 350 degrees.

2. In skillet, brown pork roll briefly in olive oil, then remove pork roll from pan. Add celery, onion, and green pepper and cook over medium heat until vegetables are tender. Set aside.

3. Bring water to a boil in a large sauce pan. Add soup mix and cook on medium heat for 5 minutes or until the noodles are tender. Stir in canned soup, pork roll, rice, and vegetables.

4. Pour mixture into greased baking dish. Cover with foil and bake for 40 minutes. Remove foil. Combine butter and bread crumbs and spread over top of casserole, then bake for 10 to 15 minutes or until topping is golden brown. Allow to rest for 10 minutes before serving.

VARIATIONS

FOR ADDED COLOR, USE HALF A RED PEPPER AND HALF A GREEN PEPPER INSTEAD OF AN ENTIRE GREEN PEPPER.

....

ADD 4-OUNCE CAN OF MILD CHILES, DRAINED AND CHOPPED, WHEN COMBINING INGREDIENTS.

....

SPINACH AND PORK ROLL BAKE

Get your vegetables and protein in one dish with this easy, flavorful casserole that is a great weeknight supper.

1 pound pork roll, chopped into bite-size pieces
////
1 tablespoon oil
////
½ cup onion, peeled and chopped
////
1 jar (7 ounces) red peppers, drained and chopped, divided use

1 package (10 ounces) frozen spinach, thawed and squeezed dry
////
1 cup all-purpose flour
////
¼ cup Parmesan cheese, grated
////
1 teaspoon dried or 1 tablespoon fresh basil

Salt to taste
////
8 eggs
////
2 cups milk
////
1 cup shredded provolone cheese

MAKES 6 SERVINGS

1. Grease a 3-quart baking dish. Preheat oven to 425 degrees.

2. Cook pork roll briefly in skillet, then remove meat and place in greased baking dish. Add onion to and sauté until translucent.

3. Combine onion and pork roll in greased baking dish and top with half of the red peppers and all of the spinach.

4. Combine flour, Parmesan cheese, basil, and salt in a mixing bowl. Whisk the eggs with the milk and stir into flour mixture. Pour over the spinach.

5. Bake uncovered for 15 to 20 minutes or until a knife inserted in the center comes out clean. Top with the rest of the red peppers and the provolone and bake for 3 to 5 more minutes or until the cheese is melted. Let stand for 5 minutes before serving.

SLOW COOKER CHICKEN AND PORK ROLL STEW OVER RICE

On a cold winter's night, homemade chicken stew is always a welcome meal. Give yours a little something extra by adding chopped pork roll.

2 pounds boneless chicken

Salt and pepper

1 tablespoon olive oil

1 medium onion, peeled and minced

3 cloves garlic, peeled and minced

1 can (8 ounces) tomato sauce

Pinch of crushed red pepper flakes, or to taste

Dash of Worcestershire sauce

3 tablespoons all-purpose flour

3½ cups chicken broth, divided use

2 bay leaves

2 cans (15 ounces) cannellini beans, drained then rinsed

1 pound pork roll, cut into bite-size pieces

1 cup long-grain rice, cooked according to package directions

MAKES 8 SERVINGS

1. Heat the olive oil in a large skillet over medium-high heat. Chop the chicken into bite-size pieces, season with chicken with salt and pepper, and transfer to the skillet to sear for 2 to 3 minutes on each side. Don't worry about cooking the chicken all the way through; this is just to seal the flavor inside.

2. Add the chicken to the slow cooker.

3. Reduce the heat under the skillet to low and add the garlic and onions. Cook just until beginning to brown.

4. Stir in the tomato sauce and red pepper flakes, and cook 1 minute. Stir in the flour and cook until the mixture just begins to thicken, creating a roux.

5. Slowly whisk in   cup of broth, scraping up any browned bits from the bottom of the pan. Gradually whisk in another cup of broth and mix until smooth.

6. Transfer mixture to a slow cooker and add remaining broth and bay leaves. Cover and cook on low, 3 hours. Uncover and add cannellini beans and pork roll and cook for 1 hour longer.

7. Prepare rice according to package directions.

8. Discard the bay leaves. Spoon stew into shallow bowls over hot rice and serve.

VARIATIONS

ADD 8 OUNCES OF CHOPPED SPINACH DURING FINAL 10 MINUTES OF COOKING.

· · · · · · · · · · ·

SKIP THE RICE AND INSTEAD SERVE OVER STEW DUMPLINGS. DURING THE FINAL 12 MINUTES OF COOKING, SPOON DUMPLING DOUGH INTO THE SLOW-COOKING STEW. COVER AND ALLOW TO COOK UNTIL DUMPLINGS NO LONGER APPEAR DOUGHY.

· · · · · · · · · · ·

MEATY PASTA SAUCE WITH PORK ROLL

Ground beef and pork roll make a flavorful and hearty combination in this updated tomato sauce.

1 to 2 tablespoons olive oil

2 cups pork roll, cut to ½-inch dice

1 pound ground beef

½ medium onion, peeled and diced

½ green pepper, diced

1 jar (24 ounces) marinara sauce

⅓ cup hearty red wine

Salt and pepper to taste

MAKES 6 SERVINGS

1. Heat 1 tablespoon olive oil in large pot or Dutch oven. Add the pork roll and cook briefly, just until brown. Remove from pan and set aside, leaving oil in pan.

2. Brown the ground beef. Remove beef from pan. Set aside with pork roll.

3. Add more oil to the pan if needed, and sauté the peppers and onions until they begin to soften.

4. Add the marinara, wine, and meats. Simmer on low for about an hour, stirring frequently. Serve over your favorite pasta.

VARIATION

IN STEP 3, ADD CUP FRESH MUSHROOMS THAT HAVE BEEN CLEANED AND CHOPPED.

HOMEMADE BEEF AND PORK ROLL MEATBALLS

These meatballs have a little taste of Jersey with the addition of pork roll.

½ pound pork roll, grated, ground or finely chopped

////

1 pound ground beef

½ cup grated Parmesan cheese

////

½ cup seasoned bread crumbs

1 tablespoon chopped fresh parsley

////

1 large egg

////

1 clove garlic, peeled and minced

MAKES 18 MEATBALLS

1. Preheat oven to 375 degrees. Combine all ingredients and shape into 18 meatballs.

2. Place the meatballs in a 13x9-inch baking pan. Bake for 25 minutes. Serve with your favorite tomato sauce over pasta.

VARIATION

ADD 1 TABLESPOON CHOPPED CANNED ROASTED RED PEPPERS OR A 4-OUNCE CAN OF CHILES, DRAINED, FOR COLOR AND FLAVOR.

....

PORK ROLL, CORN, AND NOODLE CASSEROLE

With noodles and vegetables, this meaty, filling main dish needs no adornment or side dishes.

2 cups uncooked egg noodles

2 pounds pork roll, cut into bite-sized cubes

1 tablespoon oil

2 medium onions, chopped

2 cans (15¼ ounces each) whole kernel corn, drained

2 cans (10¾ ounces each) condensed cream of mushroom soup

½ teaspoon salt

½ teaspoon pepper

MAKES 8 SERVINGS

1. Grease a 3-quart baking dish. Preheat oven to 350 degrees.

2. Cook the noodles according to package directions. Drain and set aside.

3. Add oil to large skillet and cook pork roll briefly. Remove pork roll and add onions, cooking long enough to soften.

4. Combine pork roll, onions, corn, mushroom soup, salt, and pepper and pour into greased dish. Cover and bake for 30 minutes. Uncover and bake for 15 minutes more.

SPRINKLE ½ CUP BREAD CRUMBS OVER TOP OF CASSEROLE FOR FINAL 15 MINUTES OF BAKING.

. . . .

SUBSTITUTE 1½ CUPS FROZEN PEAS (THAWED) FOR ONE CAN OF CORN.

. . . .

IF YOU HAVE LEFTOVER GRILLED CHICKEN, CHOP IT UP AND ADD IT WHEN YOU ADD THE SHRIMP.

· · · · · · · · · ·

ADD ½ CUP CHOPPED OKRA WITH PORK ROLL.

· · · · · · · · · ·

PORK ROLL JAMBALAYA

Cajun seasoning and hot sauce make this dish a favorite for those who love spicy foods.

1 tablespoon oil

1 large onion, peeled and coarsely chopped

1 small green bell pepper, cleaned and chopped

3 garlic cloves, peeled and minced

2 cups pork roll, coarsely chopped

2 cups uncooked rice

1 quart chicken broth

1 can (14½ ounces) tomatoes, coarsely chopped, including juice

1 can (8 ounces) tomato sauce

2 teaspoons Cajun seasoning

1 teaspoon hot sauce or to taste

1 pound unpeeled medium-size fresh shrimp

3 tablespoons chopped green onions

MAKES 6 TO 8 SERVINGS

1. Sauté onion and bell pepper in oil in a large pot, 2 to 3 minutes or until tender. Add garlic, and sauté briefly, about 1 minute.

2. Add pork roll, rice, and chicken broth to pot. Bring to a boil; cover, reduce heat to low, and simmer 20 minutes. Stir in tomatoes, tomato sauce, Cajun seasoning, and hot sauce.

3. Peel the shrimp and devein, if you prefer. Add shrimp and green onions to pot. Cook 2 to 3 minutes or just until the shrimp turn pink.

BAKED BEANS WITH PORK ROLL

Old-fashioned baked beans get a new twist with the addition of pork roll.

2 cups dry white beans

1 cup pork roll, diced

1 tablespoon oil

1 small onion, peeled and sliced

⅓ cup molasses

½ cup brown sugar

2 teaspoons salt

2 teaspoons dry mustard

¼ teaspoon ground ginger

Dash of black pepper

MAKES 6 TO 8 SERVINGS

1. Place beans in a large bowl and cover with water. Cover with foil or a towel and allow the beans to soak overnight on the kitchen counter.

2. At least 8½ hours before serving, drain the beans and put them in a large pot. Cover with fresh water, bring to a boil and simmer until tender, about 30 minutes.

3. While beans are cooking, preheat oven to 300 degrees. Grease a large casserole dish. Briefly brown the pork roll in the oil and remove to the casserole dish. Add onion to pork roll pan and cook for 2 to 3 minutes, until softened.

4. Drain the water from the beans, reserving the cooking water for possible later use. Add beans to the casserole dish along with onion, molasses, brown sugar, salt, mustard, and pepper. Stir to combine.

5. Bake, covered, for 8 hours, stirring often. If the beans become dry, add the reserved cooking water, a little at a time.

SERVE WITH SLICES OF HEARTY WHOLE GRAIN BREAD AND PLENTY OF BUTTER.

SPAGHETTI AND PORK ROLL FRITTATA

This one-pan treat is a meal in itself with its combination of spaghetti, pork roll, eggs, and tuna.

2 tablespoons bread crumbs

////

Butter for pan

////

3 tablespoons olive oil, divided use

2 garlic cloves, peeled and minced

////

½ cup pork roll, chopped

////

2 cups spaghetti, cooked al dente and drained

1 (3.5-ounce) can of tuna in oil

////

2 tablespoons fresh parsley, chopped, or ½ teaspoon dried

////

6 large eggs

MAKES 4 TO 6 SERVINGS

SKIP THE TUNA, IF
YOU PREFER.

ADD 2
TABLESPOONS
BLACK OR GREEN
PITTED OLIVES
IN STEP 3.

1. Preheat the oven to 375 degrees. Generously butter a 9-inch oven-proof skillet (cast iron works well) and spread bread crumbs across the bottom.

2. In a separate large skillet, combine 2 tablespoons of the oil and garlic and cook until the garlic begins to soften. Add pork roll and brown lightly.

3. Remove the skillet from the heat, add the spaghetti, and toss in the oil, garlic, and pork roll. Add the tuna and parsley. Transfer ingredients to the prepared oven-proof skillet.

4. Using a whisk, beat the eggs lightly until blended and pour over the spaghetti mixture. Top with a drizzle of oil.

5. Bake until the edges are brown and frittata is set is the center, about 25 minutes. Remove from oven and allow to cool briefly, then remove to platter where it can be cut into wedges.

INDEX

ABOUT CIDER MILL PRESS BOOK PUBLISHERS

Good ideas ripen with time. From seed to harvest, Cider Mill Press brings fine reading, information, and entertainment together between the covers of its creatively crafted books. Our Cider Mill bears fruit twice a year, publishing a new crop of titles each spring and fall.

VISIT US ON THE WEB AT

www.cidermillpress.com

OR WRITE TO US AT

12 Spring Street
PO Box 454
Kennebunkport, Maine 04046